Coaching Yourself to Leadership

Five Key Strategies for Becoming an Integrated Leader

Ginny O'Brien

HRD Press, Inc.
Amherst, Massachusetts

Published by: HRD Press, Inc.
22 Amherst Road
Amherst, MA 01002
1-800-822-2801
(U.S. and Canada)
1-413-253-3488
1-413-253-3490 (Fax)
www.hrdpress.com

ISBN 0-87425-869-3

Cover design by Eileen Klockars
Production services by Anctil Virtual Office
Editorial services by Sally Farnham

For my daughter Seana and my sister Maureen

Table of Contents

Acknowledgments

I am deeply indebted to all the people I have met on my journey who have supported me and helped me to develop and grow. But most of all I am indebted to my clients, from whom I learn all the time. The stories and case studies in this book are based on their experiences, but the names and details have been changed to protect their identities. I have also used artistic license at times and altered some of the experiences and stories in order to make my points more clearly. I am always humbled by my work and by the ways in which I see people make changes as they strive to develop themselves. Through reading their stories and mine, I hope you, the reader, will be able to take away at least one powerful nugget of wisdom that will assist you in your own growth as a leader.

Introduction

If you look at the vast range of leadership books on the market, you will see that most of them are written by men, which means that definitions of leadership are influenced by characteristics and traits that men see as important. I view leadership through feminine eyes and have made my judgments, working with both women and men, about what constitutes an effective leader. I use the term "integrated leader" to describe people who have integrated competencies from three main domains of leadership and who have integrated both masculine and feminine elements of strength into their leadership styles.

In the model I use to coach people, leadership develops internally beginning with a deep understanding of the self, and blossoms externally from learning how to empathize, engage, and communicate with others.

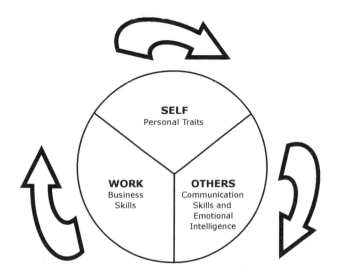

This integrated model of leadership addresses three domains in which the individual develops in relationship to the self, to others, and to work. It is an iterative, not a linear, model that the leader cycles through as he or she continually develops and grows.

In *Coaching Yourself to Leadership*, I've identified five key strategies that I believe are essential for becoming a leader: be authentic, be visionary, be emotionally intelligent, be an assertive communicator, and be connected to others through relationships and alliances. All of these strategies are developed within the domains of self and others, where most of my work as a coach takes place. Development of business skills in the domain of work relies to a large degree on personal growth, the development of emotional intelligence, and the ability to communicate assertively. Therefore, in this book, as in my coaching practice, I'm going to share ways for you to grow in all three domains— self, others, and work—by talking about ways in which you can coach yourself as you develop on a personal and interpersonal level. For example, the ability to think and plan strategically and develop goals and priorities comes from being strategic with one's own self-development, with seeing possibilities, with creating vision, with being persistent and driving toward results. Strategic capabilities also stem from understanding how others think—clients, customers, suppliers, vendors, and competitors. Although much business knowledge can be derived from reading and formal training, it is also acquired by interacting with other people, being curious about their intent and their motives, and knowing how to ask questions and listen to the answers. Emotional intelligence and communication skills are also critical for most problem solving because getting results from other people requires us to know how to manage them and build trust, analyze what they need, and make good judgments decisively and confidently. So the advice, tools, and information on ways to enhance your skills in the domains of self and others will help you advance in the domain of work.

Each of the five chapters centers on one of the five key strategies and the specific knowledge that you'll need to develop your leadership ability. Chapter One, "Be Authentic: Work According to Your Values," lays the foundation. It focuses on how to identify your core values so that you can lead with authenticity, and, for women, this might mean leading in a different way than men do. But whether you're a man or a woman, knowing and honoring what you value most will help to keep you grounded in your own integrity. In this chapter, you'll find ways to examine and change beliefs and behaviors that prevent the leader in you from fully emerging, and you'll discover practices that will enable you to become a positive, authentic leader.

The second chapter, "Be Visionary: Know Where You Want to Go and How to Get There," centers on developing even more self-knowledge. It calls for you to build your visionary capabilities and to examine your strengths so that you can leverage them to achieve your visions. In this chapter, you'll learn how to create goals for yourself, to assess your ability to take risks, identify possibilities and opportunities, and stretch yourself. And you'll discover how to plug into your intuition and use your smarts to create strategies that will enhance your leadership and help you and your team to achieve your goals.

In Chapter Three, "Be Emotionally Intelligent: Build Your EQ Muscles," a shift takes place as you begin moving away from the focus on your "self" to focusing on others. In order to be an integrated leader, you must understand and manage your own emotions and the emotions of others. As a leader, you'll be called on to influence people above you, below you, and around you. This chapter offers tools, tests, and exercises to help you get a handle on how to build trust, empathize with others, operate with respect, manage differences, make good judgments, and become a role model for others.

Chapter Four, "Be Assertive: Know How to Communicate Effectively," continues to look at emotional intelligence as it relates to communication. In order to be a truly effective leader, you must know how to communicate your values, vision, and goals so that they are heard, understood, and responded to. In this chapter, we'll examine differences in communication styles. You'll find practices and techniques for making yourself a more assertive leader who knows how to communicate in skillful ways, successfully influencing, motivating, and negotiating with others to achieve desired goals and arrive at mutually satisfying solutions.

Finally, in Chapter Five, "Be Connected: Build Strategic Relationships," we complete the shift from focusing on the self to focusing on others. This chapter centers on the importance of others in developing your leadership ability. The paradox of leadership is that it develops within, yet its real power is derived from without. You'll discover how to identify, build, and nurture mutually beneficial relationships up, down, and across your organization. This chapter provides basic networking tools as well as guidance on managing your boss and building and motivating your team.

Each chapter builds on the one that precedes it, yet stands on its own and can be used independently to build skills in that area. Values provide the grounding force from which vision can emerge, yet values and vision on their own do not ensure leadership. Emotional intelligence—a deep understanding of the self, of others, and of the environment—is necessary to put values and vision in a context that can be embraced. Emotional intelligence is also necessary so that we can frame our communications in a way that enables people to hear us. Without emotionally intelligent, assertive communication, the necessary relationships with customers, clients, employees, vendors, suppliers, team members, and management won't be successfully developed and nourished. Developing in one area opens the way to developing in the next.

My goal in writing *Coaching Yourself to Leadership* isn't to help you become the next Jack Welch or Anne Mulcahy, (being a great leader doesn't mean you have to get to the top), but rather to provide you with guidance, exercises, tools, and information to help you become an integrated leader who can make work more happy, fulfilling, and productive for yourself and those you lead.

CHAPTER ONE
Be Authentic:
Work According to Your Values

"Can you name your two most important core values?" I ask this question in workshop after workshop, and it's amazing to me how many people are not in touch with themselves and can't come up with an answer.

Leadership develops from within, and it grows through a process of self-discovery. Integrated leaders know who they are and what they want. They understand themselves well and honor their own core values. These values anchor them as they move through their careers, guiding them in everything they do.

Yet in this busy, fast-paced world, people often feel overwhelmed with their workloads and don't think they have the time to reflect on themselves.

Who Are You?

Reflecting on who you are and what you care about, and identifying and honoring your core values are the first steps to take in coaching yourself to become an integrated leader. It's essential to do your inner work and unlock the constraints that keep you from knowing and honoring your deeper self. Acting on core values is particularly important during times of chaos and uncertainty, when the only thing you can be certain about is who you are. If you are not certain about yourself, you will transmit this sense of confusion and doubt to others, negatively impacting not only your ability to influence and guide others, but also your ability to make good choices.

So first and foremost, you need to understand who you are as a person. What do you believe? What do you value? Being an integrated leader means learning how to operate from a position of authenticity—being truthful with yourself and living up to your own highest values. If you want to lead and influence others, then you need to be conscious of your actions, values, and beliefs, and be aware of your behaviors and how they affect you and others. When you operate without integrity and authenticity, without conscious core values to anchor you, you can get out of balance and lose your power and ability to lead.

Moreover, if your core values are not being honored, you will not feel happy and fulfilled. If your core values are not being acknowledged and integrated into your work, your ability to lead will be stymied because you will feel disconnected and de-energized in some way. This sense of disconnection is particularly challenging for women because historically, organizations have not been structured around feminine values. This is the real reason why many women leave organizations right at the point when they could take on greater leadership roles: They feel disconnected and can no longer tolerate the degree to which their values are not being honored in their companies. They no longer have the energy to play the game.

Research on women's strategies for success that I conducted back in the mid-1990s revealed that women value achievement of goals, happiness, balance, relationship, and the ability to make a difference. This contrasts with traditional "masculine" values of goal achievement, power through position, and financial reward. Research studies in 2004 that examined motivating factors in executive men and women had similar findings. Men were motivated by career development, professional recognition, and financial compensation, while women were motivated by relationships, the quality of customer focus, and communication with colleagues. However, other recent research shows that the values of Generation X men and women are becoming more closely aligned. Perhaps value shifts are taking place. In any case, one of the major goals of an organization should be to make sure that its values are inclusive so that all people can feel honored and connected.

Your goal should be to know what *your* values are, and to make sure that they are aligned with your company's values so that you will feel connected and have the energy to lead.

Reflecting Your Way to Authenticity

In today's hectic world, our lives swirl around us, leaving us with the perception that we have no time to attend to our own needs. But you can begin changing your perceptions if you allow yourself some amount of time each day, even if it's only for five minutes, to sit alone and reflect on what's happening. Self-awareness develops through self-observation. By tuning into your emotions and behaviors and noticing the way you are feeling and acting, you can begin to uncover the real *you*.

What makes you happy? What drives you crazy? What do you care about most in life? Who are the people whom you enjoy being with? Who brings out the best in you? In what kind of environment do you flourish? Who are the people and what are the situations that touch your hot buttons and cause you to react negatively? What are the values that you cherish most?

The first step in becoming an integrated leader is to identify two or three core values, and then use them as guiding principles to determine what you will and won't do on your journey through the business world. Values serve as navigational tools. They help you determine whether you are going in the right direction, and they can anchor you if you get caught in a maelstrom of confusion. Using your values to stabilize yourself can clear up a fog of indecision created by feeling lost or not knowing which choice to make.

My Values

Let me share my own core values to demonstrate what I mean. One of my core values is to be acknowledged and respected for my intelligence. Another is to have my voice heard. Therefore, it's no surprise that I find writing and speaking rewarding. Writing books gives me a way to gain broader recognition for my intellectual abilities, and both speaking and writing provide me with a way to have my voice heard, to tell my story, and to present my version of how I see the world to a larger audience. These values are driven in part by psychology—by the family system in which I was raised and by my own personality structure created by the interplay of nature and nurture during the developmental phases of my life.

I've known since 1985 that I wanted to be a writer, but I didn't start to write my first book until 1995. During that decade, I was working in the field of public relations and marketing communications and performing well, but I didn't feel like I was doing what I was supposed to be doing and I wasn't feeling fulfilled. If you had put a list of values in front of me during that time, I would never have checked off *recognition* and *acknowledgment*, because I would have thought that those traits reflected self-centeredness or vanity. Yet when I am not recognized and valued for my unique contributions, at work or at home, I am unhappy. I left organizations that could not provide me with that kind of support without truly understanding why I was unhappy or what was compelling me to leave. I thought there was something wrong with me or wrong with the people in the organization. But the fact is that we just weren't a good fit; the values of those particular organizational systems didn't allow my values and talents to flourish.

Some of my clients have struggled with the same dilemma. When I work with them to uncover the root of why they are repeatedly feeling unhappy or unfulfilled, we often discover a "values disconnect"—a misalignment between their values and the values of their organization. When your core values are not being honored, when you operate in an environment or in a relationship that doesn't allow your core values to flourish, your spirit suffers. When your spirit suffers, you can lose touch with your power. You will not find true happiness and fulfillment if you are not operating authentically—if you are not doing the kind of work that touches your soul and enables the real *you* to shine. And if you are not operating from that deeper level, you have not integrated and honored all the parts of yourself; therefore, you won't have the power and the energy to act as an effective leader.

Your self-confidence and self-esteem, necessary ingredients of leadership, grow out of authenticity. Time and again, I have seen high-potential men and women turn away from their organizations once they realized that there was no way to bring their core values into alignment with their organization's values. They were not able to lead because they could not lead with their own values. Read the case study on the following two pages to more fully understand the importance of being in touch with *your* values.

Values: The Case of Ruth

Ruth worked for a small firm that provides consulting services to Fortune 500 companies. She came to me stressed out, frustrated, and demotivated. Her work was suffering and she was getting entangled in a negative downward spiral. She wanted coaching because she was considering breaking away to start her own business in the same industry, which at first sounded like a powerful move to make.

Through coaching, Ruth realized that she was fooling herself into thinking that starting her own company would be a way to let her leadership ability emerge. That would have been a disastrous move, because she didn't have a strong enough network in place to provide her with a sufficient client base. Ruth also discovered that she really didn't want to work on her own—she needed the sociability and support of an office environment. In fact, she is someone who thrives in a collegial atmosphere.

Coaching surfaced several underlying value issues at the core of Ruth's problems. The very strengths that she brought to her work and the aspects of herself that she valued most—her nurturing, relational ways of dealing with clients and handling her projects—were being dismissed by the senior leaders who told her to perform differently. They wanted immediate results and they wanted Ruth to follow established protocols. Ruth wanted to spend time developing relationships. There was a clash between her way of working and the firm's.

(continued)

Values: The Case of Ruth *(concluded)*

In each of her past jobs, Ruth took great pride in her ability to relate to people. But when she started to get negative feedback from her bosses in this particular company, her fears and insecurities grew. All of her buttons got pushed. She was resentful that her own style, which she felt had always worked well, wasn't being honored. Her insecurities got triggered. Losing all sense of her own power, she felt locked in a no-win situation. Ruth was experiencing a "values disconnect" and her fear was gaining the upper hand.

Through coaching, Ruth was eventually able to articulate to her bosses her need to take time to develop relationships with her clients, but they held firm in their beliefs. It took a couple of months for Ruth to realize that what she wanted to happen at her office wasn't going to happen: The firm had its own way of doing business, and she didn't fit in. And that was okay. She had learned a tremendous amount by working there. Her style had been valued in other organizations and would be valued elsewhere.

Ruth began to work for a start-up organization in a different industry that provided services she deeply believed in. Her relational approach and skills were valued once again, and she soon became involved in developing new programs that called for reaching out to particular groups and building trust. By honoring her own values and integrating them into her leadership style, she not only found fulfilling work, but was able to provide leadership that was appreciated and that supported the organization's goals.

**What did you learn from Ruth's story
that you can apply to your own situation?**

Identifying Values:
Getting to the Core *You*

Core values surface through behavior. Identifying core values, however, can sometimes be tricky. Look at the following list of values, and circle five that you feel are the most important to you. You might want to circle far more than five, but force yourself to prioritize. If you have a value that's not listed, add it.

A List of Values		
achievement	creativity	perseverance
advancement	fame	personal growth
adventure	family	physical fitness
affluence	financial security	power
authority	friendship	privacy/solitude
autonomy	fun	recognition
balance	happiness	relationship
beauty	health	respect
belonging	humor	responsibility
challenge	influence	risk
change	inner harmony	security
clarity	integrity/honesty	sensuality
collaboration	intelligence	spirituality
community	intimacy/love	stability
competence	justice/fairness	status
competition	knowledge	vitality
contribution	loyalty	wealth
courage	orderliness	wisdom

The values you circled in the list are the values that you believe you hold. However, there is a difference between the values we *espouse* to have and our values in action—those we demonstrate through behavior. This next exercise, which I've adapted from the work of Sydney Rice Harrild and her unique process "The Paper Room," will help you identify the values that truly form the core of who you are. Sydney has been a great mentor to me and an angel as I established my coaching business. It was she who first taught me that our peak experiences reveal what we really value.

To find out what you truly value, go to the Core Values Exercise on page 10 and write down five peak experiences in your life—events or accomplishments that turned you on and made you feel really good about yourself. A peak experience can be a one-time event or ongoing experience that gives you a feeling of happiness and fulfillment. For example, one unique peak experience in my own life was being accepted into graduate school at Harvard. Another ongoing peak experience is being a mother.

After you have written down your five experiences, go back and explain what it is about them that made you feel so good. What characteristics of the experience account for your feelings? In my case, getting into Harvard was an acknowledgment of my intellectual skills. I shot for what I considered to be the top and made it, demonstrating that I had the intellectual ability to get in the door of what many consider to be the world's most prestigious university.

Now write down five of your hot buttons. What is it that really triggers you and makes you see red? Identify five things that cause you trouble. Then, identify what it is in each hot button that gives you so much trouble, and write these down in the second section. What is it about your hot buttons that gets you mad? For example, I have problems with narcissistic people who only focus on themselves and can't hear what I'm saying. I find it extremely frustrating to try to relate to people who can't relate back in a way that

Core Values Exercise

Write down five peak experiences in your life. Describe the characteristics of those experiences that made them so wonderful for you.

1.

2.

3.

4.

5.

Write down five of your "hot buttons"—situations, attitudes, or behaviors that really aggravate you and make you angry. Describe what makes them so annoying.

1.

2.

3.

4.

5.

Working with a partner, examine your peak experiences and your hot buttons to find underlying similarities and patterns. Look at the language you use to describe your experiences, and pick out repeated words and phrases. You should be able to identify at least two core values that are of the most importance to you in terms of finding happiness and fulfillment.

makes me feel that I'm heard and that my ideas are recognized and valued. People don't have to agree with me, but I need to know that they respect me enough to try and understand what I'm thinking and feeling. Narcissistic people don't do that.

When you have finished writing your descriptions, compare what you wrote about your peak experiences with what you wrote about your hot buttons. What patterns can you identify? A hot button is really the flip side of a value; you get mad because a value that is important to you is missing.

In my case, getting into Harvard met my need for recognition. I was acknowledged for my intellectual abilities. It validated me. When I deal with narcissistic people, I don't get that validation and recognition, and I'm left feeling unacknowledged and frustrated. While many of us do not like narcissistic people, they are particularly troublesome for me.

This exercise is more effective if you do it with another person. Have the person working with you look at what you've written and identify words and phrases that you've repeated in your descriptions. Many of us have the same core values—recognition, achievement, relationship, for example—but how we *describe* those values reflects more specifically what we truly honor and need. Others might see getting into Harvard as the goal in and of itself, but for me the achievement wasn't as important as the acknowledgment that maybe I really am smart.

If you talk with a friend or colleague about your peak experiences and hot buttons, you will be able to "hear" yourself better. It is also a prime opportunity to learn about your patterns through someone else's eyes and ears. We sometimes get so lost in our own mental model of the world that we literally can't see the forest for the trees. We need someone else to help us make connections that we can't see ourselves.

You should be able to identify at least one or two core values through this exercise, and you can trust that the values you'll uncover are extremely important to you. You *need* them in your life to feel happy and fulfilled, and you *need* to honor them in your work, or you won't be integrated. If you don't honor them, your leadership will be negatively impacted.

After you have completed this exercise, go back to the List of Values on page 8 to see if you circled these same values. If you did, you do know yourself well! Ask yourself if these values are being integrated into your working life. If they're not, then begin reflecting on what you need to do to get them integrated. Do you need to change your beliefs or perceptions? Your behaviors and habits? The way you interact with people? Or do you need to change your environment or the people with whom you surround yourself? Answering these questions will help you to see what you must begin doing to give the leader within you the energy to grow and develop.

Beliefs Can Make or Break You

Just as you need to be in touch with your values, you also need to identify and be in touch with your deeply rooted beliefs, because they also shape who you are and drive your behavior. Rather than striving to honor and uphold beliefs, however, question your beliefs to see if they are serving you well.

Chaos and disconnection are often caused by a clash of beliefs. Look at what is happening in the world and you'll see the evidence of conflicting beliefs. On an individual level, the "disconnect" between the desire for success and effective leadership happens when old beliefs keep people locked into old behaviors. I've noticed that one of the hardest concepts for clients to get a handle on is that their beliefs do not always represent the truth.

You are probably not even aware of how your personal belief system can affect you at work or how certain beliefs prevent you from being all that you can be. On one level, those beliefs might have helped you to achieve your present level of success, but on another level, they can keep you from moving forward and allowing your leadership to grow and flourish.

One way to empower yourself and unleash your leadership is to recognize your self-limiting beliefs. Here are some common self-limiting beliefs: *It's not possible; I don't have the time; I'm not smart enough; I'm not good enough; I don't have the right credentials; If I want it done right I have to do it myself.*

These beliefs play over and over again in our minds. More than likely, they are tapes recorded from messages that we were given in our developmental years. Some people have more negative tapes than others and some people's tapes are extremely critical and harsh. I call them your "critical voice." Some coaches call them the voice of your "gremlin." Richard Carson, author of *Taming Your Gremlin*, claims that within each of us there is a gremlin who crushes our essence with disempowering, demeaning messages. Carson claims that your gremlin will use all sorts of sophisticated maneuvers to drum these messages and beliefs into your head to keep you from feeling fulfilled and happy. But the good news is that you are not your gremlin! You can learn to turn these tapes off, or at least turn the volume down. And you can change negative beliefs that keep you from unleashing your leadership and becoming the integrated leader you were meant to be.

The first step in this process of managing your critical voice and changing self-limiting beliefs is to notice what they are. As you become a more aware and astute observer, you can diminish their power over you. As an observer, you can gain a different, clearer perspective. If you are unconsciously locked in a struggle with your critical voice, you are sure to lose and to become more entangled in the negative beliefs that will drain you. So *don't* entangle yourself: Notice what's happening. Then allow yourself to feel your feelings and your fears so that you can move beyond them. Examining your messages and beliefs will help you to distinguish how they helped you in the past and how they are holding you back in the present.

When you are able to "see," you'll notice that there are more possibilities and more ways to circumvent limiting beliefs. When you see more possibilities, you will be able to make better choices. One characteristic of an effective leader is the ability to be innovative, see possibilities, and make wise choices.

Affirmations Create Possibilities

One key way to counter negative beliefs is through affirmations. An affirmation is a positive statement or meditation that helps us to envision ourselves in more powerful ways. According to quantum physics and the laws of attraction, everything in the universe (even our thoughts) is made up of energy that vibrates at different rates. Energy that vibrates at particular levels attracts similar kinds of energy. Essentially, this means that thinking about something, negative or positive, in a deep, focused, emotional way can bring it into your life. Therefore, when you are thinking positively and sending out positive energy, more positive things will happen to you.

I think of affirmations as a modern-day form of prayer, with a key difference. I was raised as a Catholic and prayer was an everyday part of my life, but the power always resided outside of me. In other words, I prayed to God or to a host of saints as though I lacked the ability to make things happen myself. I didn't "own" my own power and thus tended to pray from a negative position. *"Please don't let this happen."* This focused attention on what I *didn't* want. So, of course, the positive things I really wanted tended not to occur. In praying that way, I focused all of the energy outside of myself. My energy was full of the fear of negative outcomes.

Affirmations, in contrast, create positive energy. For example, an affirmation for someone who believes that she can't make more money might look like this: "I am smart and good at what I do, and deserve to be richly rewarded for my efforts." This statement affirms the person's beliefs in herself and creates the space for positive things to happen. Many coaches tell their clients to write down their affirmations and post them around their house or office as reminders. (The more they look at the affirmations, the more positive their thoughts will be.)

It takes concentrated attention to change beliefs and their accompanying energy and create the reality you want. The more you focus on your affirmations, the more positive energy you will emit. The more positive energy you emit, the more positive energy you attract. I believe that the positive energy you send out into the world is related to that intangible "charisma" that is so often associated with leadership.

As you repeat your affirmations, raise your consciousness and look for opportunities that will fulfill them. Remain curious and open to possibilities. Even if you were born with the tendency to see the glass as half empty or you were raised in a system that instilled that belief, you can train yourself to notice this negative tendency and shift your beliefs toward the search for positive possibilities.

Negative Beliefs Rob You of Power

Let me give you an example of the ways in which negative beliefs can disempower you. I coached several people over the past few years who came to me in what we politely call a "transition" phase—they had been laid off and were looking for a new job. One young woman in particular was really stuck; she was quite smart, had graduated from a great school, had all the right credentials, and had worked for a couple of good companies. But once she got laid off, her insecurities ran rampant. This is not that unusual, but this young woman had the opportunity to conquer the world in any way she wanted. Yet she was drowning in negative beliefs; old messages from her dysfunctional family background were controlling her. The world was against her and she was a victim. Naturally, with that kind of outlook, she ended up with recruiters who didn't particularly care about getting her a job that would really meet her needs. Instead, they threw anything at her they could, and tried to scare her into taking jobs so that they could make their commission.

I gave her homework assignment after homework assignment—activities in between coaching sessions that would help her find a company that would be right for her. But she always found a reason for not following through, and it took us several sessions before she finally saw the heart of her dilemma: Her negative beliefs clouded everything she touched. She always had a *Yes, but* "victim" answer that kept her from taking actions that would help in her job search. In order to get a job that would satisfy her, she needed to be open to being fulfilled, which meant that she needed to change her beliefs about the world and begin to look for the possibilities rather than for the barriers. She needed to be the *leader* of her own career development, not the victim.

Unraveling Your Behavior Patterns: The Story of Brian

While you are examining your own beliefs, also observe your behaviors—the two are intertwined. Look at your behavior patterns to discover whether they are helping or hindering you from getting where you want to go. All of us are shaped by a combination of nature and nurture. Some of us have had more nurturing experiences than others and some of us are naturally more capable than others. Regardless of your background, however, you can tap into the leader within you if you are more observant of yourself and can unravel what makes you tick so that if you have to you can knit yourself into the person you want to be.

Let me share this story about one of my clients to illustrate how our personal backgrounds can affect our leadership. "Brian" heads a global team of 12 people located on three continents. He is faced with numerous challenges in the fast-paced technical environment of his company, and is constantly being called on to bring people from disparate backgrounds and cultures together to respond to the needs of international clients. He has to operate simultaneously on both a global and a local level. Brian's core values, which he is very much in touch with, are *relationship* and *integrity*. He puts his people first. He is honest to the core and has a reputation as a man of trust and integrity. He was raised in a large Irish family where all the cousins and relatives live close to one another. They get together often to help each other out, celebrate together, and raise hell. When they really raise hell and start sparring with each other, Brian says that it's often his role to bring the fighting factions together.

So Brian grew up valuing connection, watching out for the other guy, believing in the sacredness of his word, and making sure that family feuds were patched up. His family background, for the most part, serves him as a leader. But when I started working with him, he was having one problem: His natural commitment to fostering relationships and watching out for others was keeping him from being fully recognized for his leadership skills. Rather than strategically positioning himself to make sure that he got the visibility he needed, his belief that he must serve his team (translation: another kind of family) kept him from seeking any limelight. He believed that he had to meet everyone's needs and put everyone else out front to help them. This created a perception that he wasn't strong enough and didn't have the executive presence (translation: willingness to fight) to make it to the top of his highly competitive company.

Once Brian was able to make the connection between his beliefs and his patterns of behaviors, the light bulbs went off. He changed his behavior and gained increased respect from his organization, all without changing his values. Brian realized that he could position himself while still supporting his direct reports. He could help them develop, yet still take the limelight when it was important to have his voice heard. He learned he needed to speak up more; it wasn't his role in this loud organization (where people jockeyed for position by out-screaming one another) to be the quiet fence-mender, like it was in his rambunctious family. He discovered ways to push back and stand his ground without having to adopt the behaviors of others.

Brian came from a loving, supportive family albeit a noisy one. His family had a positive impact on him, but it also left him with some beliefs and behaviors that he had to become more aware of in order to allow his leadership abilities to emerge fully. One way or another, our families influence our beliefs about ourselves and the world.

The Dilemma of Defensive Behaviors

If you happened to come from a family that was *less* than loving and supportive, you might very well have some negative beliefs and behaviors that you still need to overcome. Most likely, you had to put on a suit of defensive behaviors to help you survive. As you try to become a success in the business world, those behaviors can get in your way. So, it's even more important for you to recognize which of your behaviors still serve to protect you and which can cause your downfall.

Defensive behaviors can often bring about the precise results that we are trying to avoid. And, of course, what makes it even more interesting is that defensive behaviors can get easily triggered under stress, just when you most need to use your creative juices and not your defensive ones. If you experienced childhood trauma, it is particularly important that you become aware of these defensive behaviors as a first step toward gaining greater power. You need to understand the impact of the trauma and integrate it in a way that adds, not detracts, from your leadership.

Changing behavioral patterns isn't easy. Depending on the amount and extent of re-patterning you are attempting, you might need help. Therapeutic healing work as well as coaching might be necessary in order to do the deep work that is essential to reclaiming your power and supporting your growth as an integrated leader.

Feeling Small

Many women and people of color grapple with the problem of how to hold onto their power. Although the culture is changing in terms of having more diverse people in leadership roles, women and people of color have historically been the "out-of-power" group; they haven't been the leaders. Even though they might be in positions of authority now, certain situations can trigger a "memory" of not being in control or of not having power, resulting in behavior that defers to the people who have been in the "in-power" group.

A number of my women clients, all highly competent individuals who have achieved a variety of challenging goals and attained success in their careers, remarked on this phenomenon. They all feel quite confident about their abilities; yet, certain situations (which often have to do with getting their needs met from people who have authority over them) can trigger them to feel insecure and to lose their sense of themselves. Interestingly, they all seem to respond to the triggers the same way: they begin to feel "small." They forget the powerful things they have done in their lives, and instead tend to focus on the situation that is tapping into their insecurity and decreasing their self-esteem.

The trick to regaining your power and unleashing your inner leader is to be self-aware and to recognize that you are getting hooked. If you start to feel "small," it's likely that an old feeling that developed when you were younger or when you had smaller beliefs about yourself and your power is surfacing. A good way to counter old negative feelings and images is to focus on positive feelings and images. This takes practice, but once you've created a positive image and feeling that you can easily recall, you'll be able to move quickly out of that negative space and begin acting with the power and the confidence of a leader. Using positive imagery, you'll be able to learn as much from your successes as from your mistakes, because you will be able to tap back into that feeling of power that brought you success in the past. By plugging into positive, powerful memories and replaying them so that you can feel them, you get back in touch with the authentic part of yourself, which will increase your self-confidence and ability to go for it again.

Positive Imaging Exercise

The leader within you took control when it was needed in the past, and knows how to take control of situations again. Use your memories to create a powerful mental image of yourself that is based on the reality of your experience. Recall a time when you performed really well—a time when you felt powerful and proud of an achievement or the way you handled a situation. Remember in detail what happened. What did you look like? How did you feel? What was it about your behavior that created that feeling and your success?

Practice meditating on this image, seeing and feeling your confidence and your power. Repeatedly bring this image up in your mind, and allow yourself to get in touch with the feeling associated with it. You need to practice until the recalled image rapidly triggers the powerful, self-confident feeling. Then whenever you find yourself in a stressful situation that is starting to push your insecurity buttons, recall this positive image and quickly tap into the leader within you. Using this empowering visual and emotional memory will enable you to respond in a confident, powerful manner.

Authenticity Summary Steps

To become an integrated leader, make sure that you are being authentic. Honor your core values by knowing what they are and using them to guide you. Be true to yourself, and stay grounded in your own integrity. Become an observer of yourself, and of your beliefs, attitudes, and behaviors. Prevent yourself from getting trapped in negative thoughts. Pinpoint any patterns and self-limiting beliefs that need to be changed. Recognize when your critical voice is talking to you, and take actions to counter negative messages, beliefs, or behaviors. Remember to feel the power of your past successes, and be sure you integrate them into your present-day experience, allowing the leader within you to emerge.

Coaching Questions on Authenticity and Values

Answer the following questions, reflecting on what you need to do to be authentic and work according to your values.

What is your definition of success?

What brings out the best in you?

What are your core values?

Are you presently working in alignment with your core values? If not, what do you need to do to honor your values and work more authentically?

What else must you do to be authentic at work?

What are your self-limiting beliefs?

(continued)

Coaching Questions on
Authenticity and Values *(concluded)*

How can you recognize when these beliefs are hooking you?

What can you do to get unhooked and turn self-limiting beliefs into empowering beliefs that revitalize and re-energize you?

What affirmations can you create to counter negative beliefs, attract what you need, and support your leadership development?

What do your behavior patterns tell you?

What behaviors do you need to change? What steps can you take to change them?

What do you look and feel like when you are being a leader?

What triggers you to lose your power? What do you need to do to center yourself and regain confidence?

CHAPTER TWO
Be Visionary:
Know Where You Want to Go
and How to Get There

After you have discovered who you are, the next key step to becoming an integrated leader is to discover what you want. What is your vision? Integrated leaders see possibilities. Leadership requires knowing what you want so that you can create visions for yourself and others. Having a vision for yourself is essential to attract what you want and bring it into your life and your career. Having a vision for others is essential to guide them toward intended outcomes. Vision is about being intentional. Once you have a vision, you can create long- and short-term goals. With a vision, you will see how you need to position yourself, leverage your strengths, and stretch yourself. Vision enables you to develop strategies to help yourself and others move forward to achieve results.

Dream Big Passionate Dreams

The first rule of thumb is to think *BIG*. To vision is to think about making the impossible possible. History is replete with leaders who brought us to new heights because of their ability to see what others couldn't see. If you limit your vision only to goals that are within easy reach, you won't stretch yourself enough.

I've discovered in my workshops that many people simply don't put conscious effort into creating visions for themselves. When I ask the question, *"How many of you have a vision for your career and a vision for what you want to achieve this year?"* few hands go up. If you don't get in the habit of being visionary about yourself, how can you expect to have visions of where you want to take others? The more you practice putting vision to work in terms of your own development, the stronger your "vision muscle" will be when you are leading others.

To practice being visionary in a big way, start by thinking of vision as your life's purpose. What are you here to accomplish? How should you use your talents and skills? When forming your vision, honor your authenticity and create a vision that *you* want. Your personal vision should elicit the best from you, causing you to grow and learn. It should challenge you as well as stimulate your passion. Your vision should energize you.

In creating a vision for yourself, make sure it comes from within you. Just as you need to know yourself in order to identify your core values, you need to know yourself in order to create your vision. What are your passions and dreams, your gifts and talents? What turns you on and gives you energy? One of the main themes in women's definitions of success is to make a difference in the world and have a positive impact. What impact do you want to have?

A colleague of mine provides a good example of what it means to have passionate visions. When she was in her early 30s, she became a vice president at a highly prestigious New England institution. She's now in her 40s and has her own management consulting firm. As anyone in the field knows, management consulting is a highly competitive industry with many ups and downs. Several years ago, she and her husband divorced and many of her friends recommended that she rejoin the corporate world in order to gain stability and have a steady, dependable income. But her vision was to grow her business so that she could use her money to support the philanthropic causes in which she believes. In her heart and soul, she believes that her business is the way she can make a real difference in the world. Her visions have always guided her, so she stuck with her dream. Since her divorce, she has written two books, is on the lecture circuit, and her business is thriving. She didn't give in to insecurities about whether or not she would be able to make it on her own, instead she allowed her passion for her vision to fortify her. Knowing that a book would help to position her and give her a powerful marketing tool to reinforce her business, she took on the challenge of writing. Other women might have chosen the safer path—a stable, dependable job working for someone else.

Understand Your Vision and Life Purpose

When I first start working with clients, I ask them to design a vision by imagining that they are at the end of their lives and are looking back over their accomplishments. This exercise is designed to help them get in touch with their life purpose and their individual uniqueness.

Complete the exercise on the following two pages to help you identify what you feel you must accomplish by the end of your life. Looking back, what is it that you think you will want to have achieved? What will give you a feeling of fulfillment and satisfaction? What will make you feel successful? When creating a vision, think about all the elements—the kind of work that turns you on, the financial and material wealth you want, the balance you want, the kind of family life you want, the kind of friends and social/community life you want. Think about all your gifts—your skills and talents—and how you want to use them.

Vision and Life Purpose Exercise

Imagine that you are nearing the end of your life and are looking back and assessing your success. Look at each of the categories below and describe what you would have wanted to achieve in each area in order to feel that your life was successful and fulfilling. When you have finished, review what you wrote. This is the vision you should hold for yourself.

Your professional goals—the level of power and authority you achieved:

The kind of work—activities and responsibilities—that you found fulfilling:

The kind of work environment that energized you—people, place, setting, culture:

Your financial rewards—the income and financial status that you achieved:

(continued)

Vision and Life Purpose Exercise *(concluded)*

Your family life—what it looked like and felt like:

Your social life—your friends, your community, your volunteer work:

Your use of your other talents and gifts—athletic, artistic, musical, etc.:

Your physical, emotional, and spiritual well-being—how you took care of yourself:

Use this long-range, all-encompassing vision to guide you. Once you have a clearer understanding of what you want from life, it becomes much easier to create long- and short-term goals that will keep you growing and developing.

Vision and Gender

Does gender make a difference in thinking big? Research shows that when it comes to developing business, men tend to want bigger, faster-growing firms, while women seem to take a more stable, long-term approach. Neither is right or wrong: they are just different. Research on gender differences indicates that men have a tendency from a very young age to compete and try to out-do each other. Women, on the other hand, strive for relationships and equity. Historically, women have also had numerous limitations placed on them by society and their cultures. Society has changed, however, and today's younger women are less influenced by these limitations, but I often find it necessary to help my women clients articulate what their visions are and to guide them in creating larger visions for themselves. Oftentimes, their visions are murky or not well defined. They haven't thought about setting big stretch goals for themselves or creating plans for how to reach those goals.

Several women in a study I conducted in 1996 described how male mentors and men in their lives encouraged them to strive for career possibilities that they hadn't thought about on their own. As one vice president of marketing explained, "It was an eye opener." She just hadn't thought of the possibility that she could be a top executive within a Fortune 500 company until the head of her business unit pointed her in that direction.

Creating visions means focusing on possibilities. So, when you are creating a vision for your life and career, ask yourself if you have considered *all* the possibilities. What seems so impossible for you that you just haven't even considered it? What will it take for you to include that possibility in your vision? Give your creativity free reign so that you can envision extravagant scenarios and choose those that will make you feel happy and fulfilled. Regardless of the circumstances you encounter, *you* are the only person responsible for what you do and don't do, and what you achieve and don't achieve. Don't let present obstacles or past history prevent a great future. Take control. Own the vision that you want, and articulate the future that you want. An integrated leader is determined, courageous, and persistent.

Turning My Vision into Reality

Now that we've talked about this abstract concept of thinking big, how do you really make the impossible possible? One of the best books that I've read on visioning is written by Shakti Gawain. I was introduced to her work in 1994 when a colleague gave me a copy of her book *Creative Visualization*. I had had a dream about writing a book on women, but I didn't know how to turn my dream into a reality. Gawain's book introduced me to the law of attraction, which I mentioned in Chapter One, and gave me the tools I needed. Let me explain what I mean.

When we create grand visions for ourselves, we send out energy that will attract the people, resources, and situations into our lives that will give us the opportunity to make our vision real. So the process of visioning is like a magnet that attracts what you need to make the vision possible. I know this is true, because it worked for me. At the time I was given Gawain's book, I was working as the public relations director for a major social services organization in Boston, but what I really wanted was to write about women's personal and professional development. I was in my 40s and felt that time was running out. How could I possibly make the changes I wanted to make in my career? How could I write about women's career development when I had switched from the business world into the nonprofit world? I didn't have the right connections. I didn't have the right background. I considered the choices I had made in graduate school and in my career to be all wrong.

So, I took Shakti Gawain's advice and created a visualization for myself. I pictured myself smiling and confident as I addressed women's groups, holding my newly published book in my hand (I had no idea what the name of the book was or precisely what it contained—I just knew it held women's stories). I repeated an affirmation each time I visualized my future. As I remember it, the affirmation went something like, "The words that I write and the words that I speak are powerful and strong. They help to change women's lives and bring me great financial reward." Every day before I went into my office, I stopped at the chapel next door. It provided me with the space to sit and reflect without interruption, and was a calm sanctuary in the midst of a busy downtown district. I was faithful to my visualization, and never missed a day.

One of the paradoxes of visioning is that you must remain focused on your vision without demanding a particular ending. If you try to force out all the details and expect specific outcomes, you might well be disappointed. Visioning is about imagining an ideal, creating space for it to happen, and then letting go of your attachment to all the details. At the same time, you must pay attention to what's happening around you. How is the universe offering support for your vision? It's critical to remain aware of all the opportunities that come your way, and to assess each for its potential.

In my case, about nine months after I started visioning (which I think is an interesting gestational time), I received a call out of the blue from a former colleague. She invited me to come interview for a position as a writer for a new group that was forming at MIT's Organizational Learning Center. The group was offering learning labs in transformational leadership and coaching to managers working for Fortune 500 companies.

It was a pretty big risk for me to take the job because the group was just starting up and the work was new. There was no guarantee that it would be successful. My daughter was a senior in high school and was about to start college, and my husband had just lost his job. But I decided the risk was worth taking because of the people I would be able to meet at MIT. I figured that regardless of what happened, MIT would be good to have on my résumé. Integrated leadership requires us to take calculated risks, blend rational, masculine logic with feminine intuition, and fuel the combination with courage. This was a big stretch for me, but I decided to do it because I knew I wasn't going to get what I needed if I stayed where I was.

At MIT, I was introduced to the concepts of coaching and transformational leadership. These were highly intriguing subjects to me. I had once thought about becoming a therapist, but decided against it; coaching seemed a way to use those skills in settings where people were highly motivated to succeed. It was all very appealing.

The transition, however, was not easy or smooth. I was hired as a writer not as a coach. I was supposed to be more or less ghost writing for the head of the group, but we quickly realized how much we just didn't click. It was a very stressful experience and I did not last long in the job, but it gave me time to make connections with other powerful people in the organization. I consciously set out to develop relationships with a couple of key people who eventually opened doors for me, especially one man who gave me an entree into the publishing world. This led to the publication of my first two books, so I ended up fulfilling my vision after all. The route wasn't what I had expected and was not without its bumps and disappointments, but I never let go of the vision. Despite the roadblocks that I encountered, I was determined to somehow move myself forward and become a writer. In the process of doing so, I also became a coach.

The lesson here is that to turn a vision into reality you must be open to and tuned in to possible opportunities, be willing to take risks, be smart about the moves you make, be determined and persistent, and have faith in yourself.

Assessing Your Skills: How Integrated Are You?

In order to have confidence in yourself, you need to know yourself well. In Chapter One, I talked about the importance of identifying your core values, but you also have to know your strengths and your developmental areas. There are many models of leadership, but I've designed one that works well for me and my clients. It outlines the three major domains of an integrated leader. To be integrated and effective, I believe that a leader must have capabilities in each. These three domains break down as follows:

■ **Personal traits**, which refer to innate qualities and characteristics of the self

■ **Communication skills and emotional intelligence**, which deal with your ability to understand and manage your own emotions as well as the emotions of others, and your ability to communicate in ways that enable other people to understand and respond

■ **Business skills,** which pertain to the work itself

So the first domain deals with the *self*. The second deals with the self in relationship to *others*. And the third deals with the self in relationship to *work*.

Integrated leaders have a balance of expertise in each domain, but are not necessarily strong in all the components of each domain. For example, a leader might be quite passionate and visionary, but his ability to be innovative might not be as strong. He might have great ability to motivate and empower others, but might not be as skilled at negotiating. He might know how to produce results, but might not have all the industry knowledge he needs. Integrated leaders have capabilities in each domain; it's when a leader lacks balance *across* all three domains that he is most likely to fail. A leader who has great industry and market knowledge and knows how to analyze and synthesize information yet doesn't know how to build relationships or listen to customers is doomed to fail. Likewise, someone who is confident, decisive, and determined, but who doesn't know how to develop teams or get results isn't going to succeed. Integrated leaders have skills and strengths in each domain, because integrated leaders know how to manage themselves and others, as well as their business.

Easy Assessments You Can Do Yourself

Here are a couple of tools that will help you see how integrated you are as a leader. Use the self-assessment on pages 37 and 38 to get a sense of where you stand on each of the competencies within the three domains. Where are your specific strengths? What particular competencies do you need to work on to become a more highly integrated leader? How integrated and balanced are you? In what domains do your strengths show up? In what domains do your weaknesses emerge? Are you strong in business skills but weak in emotional intelligence? Or are your strengths scattered around the wheel in all domains? To be a high-performing integrated leader, you should be balanced across all three areas, averaging a score of at least four in each domain.

Integrated Leadership:
Three Domains

SELF
Personal Traits
Authentic, Confident, Courageous,
Curious, Decisive, Determined, Flexible,
High Performing, Honest, Humble,
Innovative, Intelligent, Passionate,
Responsible, Risk Taking, Self-Aware,
Visionary

WORK
Business Skills
Possess and use industry,
business, market, and
customer knowledge;
Think strategically;
Prioritize; Analyze;
Synthesize; Problem solve;
Set goals; Get results

OTHERS
**Communication Skills and
Emotional Intelligence**
Communicate assertively; Listen;
Question; Learn; Demonstrate
respect, empathy, humility, and
balance; Use intuition and good
judgment; Influence; Negotiate;
Coach; Mentor; Role model;
Empower; Delegate; Motivate;
Build trust, relationships, and
teams

Getting Feedback from Others

A mini-feedback process can also help you understand your strengths and weaknesses. We don't always see ourselves as clearly as others see us. Therefore, try to find out how different people perceive you. How do you come across to others? What do they perceive to be your strengths and weaknesses? Companies with well-developed performance

---

Integrated Leadership Competencies Self-Assessment

Rate yourself on each of the following competencies using a scale of 1 to 5. (Scale: 1 = poor, 2 = fair, 3 = good, 4 = very good, and 5 = excellent). Then find your average score for each of the three domains.

Business Skills		Personal Traits	
Achieve results	___	Be honest and ethical	___
Think strategically	___	Be self-confident	___
Plan and set goals	___	Be authentic	___
Prioritize	___	Be decisive	___
Analyze information	___	Be determined and driven	___
Synthesize information	___	Have passion for work	___
Perform well	___	Create vision	___
Solve problems	___	Be creative and innovative	___
Understand the industry	___	Have courage, take risks	___
Understand the business	___	Lead by values	___
Understand the market	___	Be flexible and adaptable	___
Understand customers	___	Be responsible	___
AVERAGE = (Total ÷12)	___	Be optimistic	___
		Be intelligent	___
		AVERAGE = (Total ÷ 14)	___

(continued)

Integrated Leadership Competencies
Self-Assessment *(concluded)*

Communication Skills and Emotional Intelligence

Operate with respect	___	Show good judgment	___
Be a role model	___	Develop trust	___
Communicate assertively	___	Build collaboration	___
Listen actively	___	Empower/develop others	___
Ask the right questions	___	Hire the right people	___
Influence others	___	Build high performing teams	___
Empathize with others	___	Build relationships with	
Coach and mentor others	___	senior management	___
Motivate others	___	Build relationships with	
Delegate	___	clients	___
Manage conflict	___	Build relationships with	
Set expectations	___	colleagues	___
Possess humility	___	Build relationship with boss	___
Be curious and a learner	___	Manage your own emotions	___
		Manage time	___
		AVERAGE = (Total ÷ 26)	___

A high potential integrated leader should average 4 in each domain. Are you stronger in one domain than in another? Use this assessment to help you focus your development efforts.

---

measurement processes often have 360-degree feedback instruments in place, but if you haven't had access to this wonderfully powerful, (but somewhat scary) means of assessing yourself, you can do this mini-feedback yourself.

The questions in the Mini-Feedback exercise on page 40 will give you a sense of how you come across to others. Here's how to use it. Target about six friends and colleagues you trust to give you honest answers. Ask each person to help you with your professional development by answering the questions anonymously. E-mail them the questions and ask them to print out their answers on a plain sheet of paper and leave it in your in-box in order to maintain anonymity. Your job is to make them feel safe enough to give you honest feedback.

Remember that you must be open to accepting their feedback *without being defensive.* Also remember that even if you find their responses objectionable or "wrong," perception is greater than reality. If enough people are in agreement about how they are perceiving you, you must be doing something to reinforce that perception. Look for any patterns in the answers, and pay attention to them. You can use that knowledge to leverage and play to your strengths and to understand the behaviors or attitudes that you need to work on changing.

Gap Analysis:
Creating Yearly Strategies for Success

Once you know where you want to go, and once you become more realistic about your strengths and weaknesses, you can develop strategies to move yourself forward and achieve your goals. Look back at your vision. Use that to help you articulate a long-term career goal for yourself. At the start of each year, check to see if this is still your long-term goal. It might or might not be. It's okay to change your vision and goals. Also check to see how you are doing in all the other areas of your life.

Then work backwards. What short-term goal (18 months to three years) will help you achieve your long-term goal? What annual goals will help you achieve your short-term goals? Remember, this is an iterative process, so each year

---

Mini-Feedback

When you first met me, what was your perception of me? In what way, if any, has your perception changed over time?

What is there about my communication style that either impresses you or that you feel needs to be changed?

What is my greatest leadership strength? Can you give me an example of a time when you were particularly impressed with my performance or my leadership?

What are the areas that you think I should pay attention to as I try to develop my leadership abilities? Can you describe a time when you wished that I had done something differently?

What can you definitely count on me for?

What would you hesitate to rely on me for?

If you had to give me one developmental goal to work on this year, what would it be?

---

you'll want to develop annual goals that will help you fulfill your short-term goals, which will help you fulfill your long-term career goal. You need yearly goals because goals that are too far into the future can get lost in space. I sometimes find it easier to break yearly goals down even further into quarterly or semi-annual goals. A small-wins approach works best, so set achievable goals within a time span that works best for you.

One of the easiest ways to get a grip on this process is to use a simple technique known as a gap analysis. A gap analysis provides a quick glimpse into the areas you need to work on. It helps you identify what you want to achieve and where you are in relationship to your ideal state. The difference between the two is the gap. A gap analysis helps you to focus on the right goals and to prioritize the areas that are most important. When you try to close the gap, think about the three domains of leadership. What personal traits, behaviors, or beliefs do you need to change or enhance? What communication skills do you need to develop or leverage? What aspect of your emotional intelligence do you need to improve? What relationships do you need to develop and nurture? What business skills or knowledge do you need to leverage or hone? You want to create goals that stretch you but that are also achievable. You can't work on everything at once. Too many goals can trip you up. Achieving the goals you set for yourself throughout the year will help to keep you motivated and on track. So be strategic in developing your plan: What will help you most at what point? Then develop SMART developmental goals (goals that are specific, measurable, achievable, relevant, and time-bound).

For each goal, create specific measurements of success, and create action steps for each measurement. I use the terms *goals, measurements of success,* and *action steps* rather than *goals, objectives,* and *tactics* because people seem to get confused about what's a goal and what's an objective, and what's an objective and what's a tactic. A measurement shows you what success will look like, whereas an action step shows you what you need to do to achieve that success or meet that measurement.

Charting Your Goals

As an example, let's say your long-term career goal is to become a general manager of a division in your company, and your short-term goal is to move into a higher-level position with global authority within the next two years. Remember, a short-term goal is a stepping-stone to a long-term goal. With that in mind, what do you need to do this year to support your short-term goal and help close the gap?

In thinking this over, you might realize that you need to develop more knowledge of the international market and acquire experience that will help you succeed in a position that has global responsibility. But as a goal, that is somewhat vague. How would you measure success? One measurement might be to get yourself on a cross-functional team that is working on issues relevant to the position you're seeking. And it might be a good idea to do that within the next six months. But what do you need to do to get on the team? An action step might be to have conversations with a number of influential leaders over the next three months who can help you get a seat on the team. Another action step might be to take a course in communication and influencing skills to help you in your conversations with people you are trying to influence.

As you think more about it, you might also realize that another measure of success might be to develop and nurture relationships with people working on international projects. They can help you build your knowledge and provide you with advice about the best positions, pitfalls, and opportunities. One action step would be to set up breakfast, lunch, or dinner meetings with people you've targeted or to ask them out for drinks after work.

Another measure that would demonstrate your understanding and knowledge is to develop the ability to articulate key global issues, challenges, and strategies. In addition to meeting with targeted people, another action step could be to read the reports produced by particular cross-functional teams or to read a specific number of journals or other relevant material on a weekly basis. In order to clearly see all the steps you need to take and how you'll measure success, develop a chart and use it like a roadmap, checking off your progress as you move forward.

Make it a practice to review this written record of your goals every year, or even every six months or every quarter. As you achieve success, be sure to set new goals, measures of success, and action steps so that you're always working on developing yourself. If you are not taking action steps or you are not meeting your measurements of success, ask yourself what's getting in your way. What's happening to keep you from moving forward? This is a good opportunity to re-examine your beliefs and behaviors to see how they might be playing into your inability to make progress toward achieving your goal.

The Goals and Actions Sample on the next two pages provides an example of one way to set up your roadmap. You might want to use an Excel spreadsheet or create another kind of table that visually works for you, but the idea is to put your goals, your measures of success, and your action steps *on paper* so that you can easily refer to them as a guide. This sample form provides only one annual goal. You'll probably have two or three, but don't overload yourself. It's better to have a couple of goals that stretch you, but that you know you can fulfill, than it is to have a slew of goals that can cause confusion about priorities and put too much on your plate. You want to create successes for yourself. Leadership is about achieving goals and getting desired results.

Goals and Actions Sample

Long-Term Goal:
Become a general manager of a division.

Short-Term (18 months to three years) Goal:
Within two years obtain a higher-level position with global authority.

Annual Goal:
Gain relevant, global experience, knowledge, and skills by the end of the year.

Measurement of Success #1:
I'll be on a cross-functional global team within six months.

Action Step #1:
Have conversations with at least six key leaders to try to influence them to get me positioned on a cross-functional global team within the next three months.

Action Step #2:
Take a course in influencing skills to help me communicate with these key people as soon as possible.

(continued)

Goals and Actions Sample *(concluded)*

Measurement of Success #2:
I'll have developed strong relationships with at least five people who are on global teams or who are known as global leaders. They'll provide me with advice and give me the heads-up on opportunities and warn me about problems or challenges. I'll know what motivates each of them and what I have to offer each of them in return.

Action Step #1:
By the end of the month, I'll have invited Sam, Joe, Al, Candy, and Lynn for breakfast, lunch, dinner, or drinks with the purpose of sharing knowledge and information. I'll continue to meet with them at least once a quarter over the course of this year.

Measurement of Success #3:
I'll be able to clearly articulate the global issues and challenges faced by the organization, and what is being done to manage each of these challenges by the end of the year.

Action Step #1:
In addition to talking with key people (as previously mentioned), I'll read the reports produced by cross-functional teams A and B.

Action Step #2:
I'll read at least two trade journals or other relevant material on a weekly basis.

Being Comfortable Outside Your Comfort Zone

Visualization is just the beginning; it's a portal into your future. But it requires that you take risks and be smart about ways to turn your vision into reality. To become an integrated leader, you must take risks and also become consciously aware of yourself and of what's happening around you. You must know how to assess the environment to determine if and how well it will support you, and figure out what steps will lead to achieving your goals.

Taking risks, however, doesn't mean plowing ahead without thinking about consequences. It means making conscious calculations about what's involved with particular moves. It means knowing your strengths and weaknesses and understanding how far you can stretch yourself without setting yourself up to fail. Generally speaking, each of us operates within a comfort zone that provides us with a sense of security and safety. Paradoxically, the power of leadership comes from having the strength to be vulnerable and from learning to be comfortable operating outside your comfort zone. Leaders are constantly expanding their comfort zones by stretching into their *learning* zones.

If risk-taking is challenging for you, ask yourself what it is that keeps you in your comfort zone. What underlying fears might be holding you back from taking risks and moving into a learning zone? Sometimes fear can be so overwhelming that we literally can't see our strengths or the possibilities that exist for us. Sometimes, the only thing we see are the barriers. If you find that risk-taking is something you need to work on, start peeling back the layers of fear to uncover the source of your anxiety.

Fear can make you tentative; it can even freeze you into inaction. You need to discover ways to handle your fear, whether you have a fear of failure, a fear of success, a fear of looking like a fool, a fear of appearing ignorant, or a fear of looking too aggressive. Each of us has a fear that has been shaped by our own personal experiences. Taking risks means confronting challenges carefully and wisely and

The Risk Bull's Eye

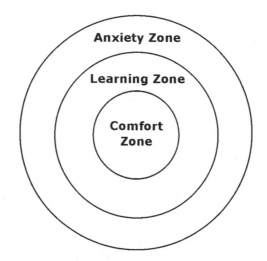

having the courage to move ahead through fear. An integrated leader knows how to work through fear. If you wait until you get rid of fear before you take action, you'll never move anywhere. Leaders are always dancing in and out of their learning zones.

Managing Your Fear

Here's a process for managing your fear and calculating the risk that's stirring the fear. First, look at the facts—lay out the situation so that you can clearly see it. Then determine the worst-case scenario. What's the worst thing that can happen to you if you take this risk? What are you most afraid of? Second, think about the opportunities that will be lost if you don't take the risk. What opportunity might you miss that will be very hard for you to recapture?

Compare the worst-case scenario with the lost opportunity. Which is truly worse? Sometimes when we examine the worst-case scenario, we discover that it's not really that bad after all. And sometimes when we examine the lost opportunity, we discover that the opportunity is simply too good to give up. So make sure that you have fully examined the situation. But don't make your decision yet: Do some more homework. Talk to a variety of people whose opinions and expertise you respect and admire. You need to hear other perspectives, because you might be blind to something you should be seeing and considering. So gather information and gain knowledge about all the facets related to the risk. Then plug in to your intuition, summon up your courage, push through your fear, and make the right decision.

If you don't go through all of these steps, you might make a choice that you will later regret. We learn by our mistakes, but some mistakes are harder to recover from than others. I believe in an abundant universe and the axiom "When a door closes, a window opens," but some opportunities are extremely rich and timely. If you miss a particularly choice one, it might be quite a while before you can recoup the loss.

My Mistakes

Let me share something that happened to me earlier in my career that will demonstrate how fear can cloud our vision when it comes to taking risks and making choices. I went to school as an adult to complete my college education. After I finished my undergraduate work, I was accepted into graduate school at Harvard and Boston University. Getting into Harvard was my ultimate goal, and I was really proud of myself when I learned I had been accepted into the program on human development. About a week after I had sent in my check and acceptance notice, I was contacted by Brandeis University and offered a fellowship in a Ph.D. program in experimental psychology. I hadn't been crazy about the program when I applied because it didn't seem like a good fit to me, but one of my undergraduate professors had suggested it.

When I was offered the fellowship, I was torn with indecision. I really wanted to go to Harvard, but if I went to Brandeis, I would have a paid fellowship. I was a divorced, single mother of a young child. Money was a big issue. In fact, one of my gremlins is a money monster who is always telling me that I won't have enough money. So, I let my "scarcity" mentality influence my decision. I ended up going to Brandeis because of the financial support the school offered.

By the end of the first semester, I was a wreck. I was in my 30s, and the other graduate students were in their 20s and far more technologically sophisticated than I. They sat down at their computers and whizzed through statistical programs that I had no idea how to run. Even though I finished the first semester with a B average, I feared I wasn't as smart as they were. The statistics course had kept me up until all hours of the night, and I imagined the years of correlation coefficients and standard deviations that would be in front of me. It was frightening. On top of that, I was an Irish, ex-Catholic divorcee who had been taught that advanced education was for men—not for women. The role that I had been presented with growing up was one of a stay-at-home mother who had no college degree. Yet here I was trying to get a Ph.D. surrounded by Jewish intellectuals who came from entirely different backgrounds. Surely, I wasn't smart enough—who was I kidding? Fear blinded me to all possibilities and limited my ability to think about the future and how I wanted it to unfold. I left the program.

I ended up getting a master's degree from Boston University's College of Communication, which offered me a partial scholarship. BU is a good school, but it's not in the same category as Harvard. I didn't end up with a paid-for Ph.D., and more importantly, I didn't study what I really wanted to study. Those decisions shaped my career and turned it in a direction that didn't make me happy. It took me a long time to set a new course and head in a direction that stimulates and fulfills me.

So, thoroughly examine your fears. Compare the worst-case scenarios with the lost opportunities. Get advice from others with expertise so that you can hear different perspectives and think about things you hadn't thought of before. Then plug in to and trust your intuition.

Learning to Trust Your Intuition

Humans have used intuition as a guide for thousands of years. Some experts claim that intuition is merely a sub-conscious way of making a quick analysis—that it is probably what remains of the warning system for danger used by the first humans. I believe that our intuition holds wisdom gained from ancient experience, as well as from our own emotional memories.

By being more aware of how your intuition works and consciously using it, you enhance your power to take risks and make difficult decisions. Lynn Robinson, author of *Divine Intuition: Your Guide to Creating a Life You Love*, says intuition can come in a variety of ways—through an image, words, thoughts, an emotion, a body sensation, a fleeting impression, or a hunch. There is no one perfect or right way, but as you practice consciously using your intuition, it will be easier and easier for you to tap in to it successfully.

As you become more familiar with and more trusting of your intuition for discovering answers and making the right choices, you gain personal power because you learned to honor your gut instincts. By tapping in to your intuition, you consciously go beyond the rational and bring all of yourself—the linear (masculine) and the holistic (feminine)—into your decision-making process. You'll know when you should step into a learning zone and take risks and when you should step back out.

Staying in a learning zone too long is just as bad as never entering one. If you overload yourself with learning, you're much more likely to push yourself into the anxiety zone and set yourself up to fail. The stress will show in the quality of your work or the quality of your health. So trust your intuition. Integrated leaders have a good sense of balance in everything they do. They're focused on reaching their goals and succeeding, but they also know when to stretch and learn, and know when too much is too much.

Transferring Skills: From the Personal to the Professional

As you develop your ability to create vision and goals for yourself, you build your strategic thinking muscles. Being able to visualize possibilities, gather information to assess risk, and plan and set goals are the same skills you need if you want to lead a team or an organization. As a leader, you must create and hold a vision for your team, understand your business and your clients, know what's happening in the marketplace, set goals, and develop strategic plans to achieve those goals, all the while trusting your intuition. As a leader, you must understand what your team is capable of achieving, what skills the team possesses, to what extent team members are able to stretch, and what can be accomplished within specific time frames. The more skilled you are at creating visions and strategic plans for yourself, the more skilled you will be when you have to do the same thing for your team.

Risk and Intuition Exercise

Try this exercise adapted from Lynn Robinson's work to assess your risks. Write a brief paragraph about a risk you might take and the worst-case scenario associated with that risk. Then write a paragraph about the lost opportunity should you not take the risk. Start with the worst-case scenario: Close your eyes and picture the worst thing happening. Ask yourself how you feel. Let yourself really *feel* it. Imagine that it is truly happening to you. Pay attention to your body. What are you feeling? Are there words or visual images that pop up for you? Repeat the exercise, picturing the lost opportunity. Which choice elicited a better response: taking the risk with a worst-case outcome, or losing the opportunity?

Worst-Case Scenario:

Lost Opportunity:

Vision and Smarts Summary Steps

The second key strategy to becoming an integrated leader builds on the first: Continue gaining self-knowledge by finding out what you want and what you're good at. Think big, and take responsibility for creating a passionate vision that embraces your life purpose. Then identify long- and short-term goals to achieve your vision, outlining the small steps that are necessary to achieve those goals. Assess the risks you will need to take, and uncover any fears that may be keeping you in your comfort zone and holding you back. Keep examining the gap between your reality and your vision, and create strategies to close the gap and achieve your goals. Determine what you need to do to close the gap, leveraging and building on your knowledge and skills. Be persistent. Use your intellect and your intuition, and be courageous.

Coaching Questions on Vision

Answer the following questions, reflecting on what you need to do to be a visionary and a strategic thinker.

What vision do you hold for your future? What can you do to make your vision bigger?

What are your long- and short-term career goals?

What are your goals for this year?

What skills do you possess? What are your greatest strengths?

What are your developmental areas? What specifically do you need to do to improve?

What steps do you need to take to achieve your goal and close the gap between your reality and your vision?

What fears hold you back from taking any of these steps or from moving out of your comfort zone?

(continued)

Coaching Questions on Vision *(concluded)*

How effective are you at using your intuition? What can you do to get more in touch with your intuition?

How much of a risk-taker are you? If you take a risk and fail, what does that mean to you?

If you take a particular risk this year, what is the worst-case scenario that can occur? What are the possible lost opportunities? What do you discover when you compare the worst-case scenario with the most significant lost opportunity?

How determined and persistent are you in reaching your goals and getting results?

How effective are you at creating vision for your team? What can you do to be more effective?

How effective are you at setting goals and developing strategies for your team or organization? What can you do to be more effective?

CHAPTER THREE

Be Emotionally Intelligent: Build Your EQ Muscles

Of all the keys to being an integrated leader, I think emotional intelligence is the most difficult for people to get their arms around. Emotional intelligence (EQ) is more abstract than the first two strategies of values and vision. These strategies focus on understanding yourself. You can figure out what you value by thinking about your experiences, and you can determine your vision by picturing where you want to go and what you want to achieve. However, EQ calls for you to understand others as well as yourself. Basically, emotional intelligence is the ability to be intelligent about your own emotions and the emotions of others. Without the proper amount of emotional smarts, you simply won't be able to communicate well or build relationships.

If you are emotionally intelligent, you understand yourself well and know how to control your own emotions and behaviors—you know how to reign in your feelings and channel them effectively. As a leader, you should be a role model for how you want other people to behave. If you can't manage your own emotions, why would you expect others to manage theirs? An emotional breakdown on your part—whether it comes in the form of yelling, loss of confidence, or crying—sends a message that as a leader you have lost control. If you have lost control, what will happen to your team? Who will direct them? When you lose your composure, you create the impression that you are not strong enough to handle difficult situations. Team members can lose their sense of security, and the situation can become even more stressful for them. It's your job to balance negative news and stressful conditions with vision and hope for good outcomes, and it is your responsibility to provide strategies to achieve those outcomes. You can develop greater EQ by discovering what triggers you to lose control, and then learn techniques to help you manage your emotions better. If you don't know how to manage emotions and relationships, you might be the smartest person in your organization in terms of intellect or technical ability, but you're not going to have the kind of leadership ability it takes to succeed.

If you are emotionally intelligent, you are also able to connect with people on an emotional level; you understand their emotions and know how to interact successfully with them. Having EQ enables you to build bridges to others. Intuitively you know how to deal with all kinds of situations and all kinds of people. Emotional intelligence enhances your ability to influence others because you understand what motivates them. When you can see below the surface of other people's behavior, you can adapt more quickly and respond more appropriately to them. So, to be emotionally intelligent means you have a high degree of self-awareness and control *and* a high degree of awareness and understanding of others.

EQ at Work:
Maintaining Emotional Control

Have you ever had to work with someone you really couldn't stand? The very sight of the person gets under your skin. One word out of her mouth and your bells are ringing and you are ready to fight! After encounters with her, you ruminate on all the ways you are going to get back at her for the bad things she has done to you—all the clever jabs that are going to leave her smarting, all the ways you are going to one-up her and show her *your* power. If this sounds familiar, you are wasting your energy and demonstrating that you need to improve your emotional intelligence.

Emotional intelligence develops over time and grows with experience. Some people are naturally more emotionally intelligent than others, but each of us can take steps to improve our EQ. The challenge is to maintain emotional intelligence on a consistent basis so that when you are embroiled in an emotionally charged, negative situation, you can handle it astutely. It's easier to be understanding of others and to see their point of view when you aren't directly affected, but when you feel wronged or in danger, it's much harder to take an objective look at the other person. However, if you can automatically put yourself in another person's position (even in the heat of the moment) and identify what she is feeling and why, you will be able to relate to what she is emotionally experiencing. This in turn can help you figure out how to interact more effectively, how to deepen understanding and trust, and how to move toward your goals.

When you find yourself in difficult situations with other people, force yourself to answer the following questions: *What does this person need? What does this person fear? What does this person want?*

Vacillating Between Extremes

I've noticed that once people's buttons get pushed, they often respond by vacillating between two extremes. They either retreat, completely walling themselves off in the hope that the situation will somehow correct itself, or they act out aggressively. Either behavior is a set-up for failure.

If you shut down and retreat, you open up space for the other person (who is probably not displaying much emotional intelligence either) to do damage to you. When you retreat and close other people out, it's as if you have pinned a sign on yourself that can be interpreted a variety of ways, all of them negative: "I'm better than you, and I don't like you," or "I'm busy, and you're not important enough for me to deal with."

Moreover, when you're not engaged with others, people can't get an accurate reading on you, and you, in turn, can't get an accurate reading on them. When you're not engaged and don't know what's going on, you can't contribute effectively. If you close down, you allow yourself to be excluded from key groups and happenings; you lose your ability to stay in the ring, which puts you out of the loop. Shutting down leaves you vulnerable, and certainly does nothing to change the situation.

On the other hand, if you erupt like Mt. Vesuvius, you give the other person ammunition to accuse you of unprofessional behavior or label you as too emotional. Daniel Goleman, who popularized the concept of emotional intelligence, writes in *Working with Emotional Intelligence*, "Out-of-control emotions can make smart people stupid." Yelling at someone and calling them names might make you feel momentarily powerful, but the surge of pleasure you're feeling probably stems from some childhood experience when calling other kids names made you feel like you were somehow powerful. Moreover, when you scream and yell, you contribute to an unhealthy and possibly chaotic situation. Your job as a leader is to maintain a healthy and calm environment even in the midst of crisis.

If you're a woman and you sometimes erupt with frustration or screams of anger, you are more likely than a man to be criticized and accused of being over-emotional, particularly in a male-dominated environment. Because the pitch and tone of women's voices are higher and different from men's, it is already easy for men to "hear" women as more emotional than they really are. If you cry, you can be seen as needy. Tears at work confuse and scare men; their paternal instincts get triggered and they don't know what to do. One outcome is that they'll want to take care of you; another is that they'll want to avoid you. Neither outcome is good: You don't want men *or* women feeling as though they need to take care of you and you don't want anyone avoiding you.

One way or the other, you lose power if you shut down or scream out. When you are disempowered, you lose your ability to lead.

So, how do you handle these situations? When you are dealing with people who push your buttons, step back and take an objective look at what's happening. Ask yourself some more questions: What's going on here? Why am I feeling the way I do? What am I doing to contribute to this situation? Get in touch with your own emotions. Where are they coming from? What is it that *you* need?

Understanding Your Emotions: The Story of Rose

One of my clients, whom I'll call Rose, presents a good illustration of the effort it takes to go below the surface and discover the source of emotional distress. Rose had a wonderful relationship with her old boss. He was a great mentor to her and helped her develop her career. He was always there for her. He understood her personality and he supported her when she made mistakes.

When her new boss came on board, Rose had a lot of problems adjusting. She didn't like his style. She questioned his competence. And she didn't keep her feelings a secret. Rose has a temper that gets triggered when she's feeling abandoned or despondent, but she didn't know that when we started working together. All she knew was that she couldn't stand her new boss.

When good relationships in the workplace change due to a promotion, a move, or some other kind of transition, there is a sense of loss. And accompanying that loss are feelings of sadness, anger, and resentment. During these transitions, unless you can get hold of your feelings, acknowledge them, and provide yourself with a safe space to vent them, you're likely to trip yourself up.

In Rose's case, she hadn't realized the degree to which she was attached to her old boss. She also didn't realize the degree to which she was resenting her new boss. She didn't want a new boss and she found fault with everything he did. She sometimes responded to requests that seemed extreme or unreasonable with blunt disagreement, laced with sarcasm and anger.

As I listened to Rose describe all the things her boss was supposedly doing wrong, I asked her to stop for a minute and re-focus. Rather than talking about what was going on with him, I asked her what was going on with her. As I kept prodding, a light bulb finally went off—Rose realized this really was about her, not about him.

Focusing on his annoying behaviors wasn't helping her. She needed to shift her focus away from criticizing her new boss, and allow herself to feel her own sadness and anger. She needed to get in touch with her authentic self and her emotional feelings. Until she gave herself some space to grieve, she wasn't going to have room for a new relationship to grow.

We designed several interventions to help her get grounded and to become a better observer of her feelings and behaviors. First, she agreed that each time her new boss made a request or a comment that triggered a negative emotional reaction, she would take a deep breath without responding and ask herself, *What's really bothering me?* By giving herself some time to pause and reflect, she became more aware of what she was thinking and feeling, and this kept her from responding inappropriately. Within a short period of time, she was able to understand her feelings better and view her new boss from a different perspective. No matter what he did, he wasn't going to be the same as her old boss—he wasn't going to take care of her in the same way. She was at a new place in her career, which required a higher level of emotional maturity.

Next, Rose began to work on developing her ability to empathize with her new boss. He was in the middle of a volatile organizational situation, and needed the support of his troops. I asked her what she would want if she were in his shoes. As she began articulating the kinds of information and support she would need, she began to see that this was precisely what she had been holding back from him. She was almost punishing him for not being who she wanted him to be.

A third intervention we designed for Rose was to identify and improve the skills that were most important to her boss. The more credibility she had, the more respect she could command. The more he recognized her worth, the more he would value her input. The more he valued her input, the more he would listen to her when she did disagree with him and the more power she would have. The more power she had, the greater ability she had to lead her team, direct her career, and find success.

When you can identify what *you* need, you will be in a better position to articulate your position. Then uncover the needs of others. What are they afraid of? What is threatening them? What do they need from you or from the work environment?

If you can figure out which emotions you're feeling and why you're feeling them, you can find ways to control your emotions and take care of yourself in a rational manner. If you can figure out which emotions others are feeling and what triggered them, you can figure out ways to help them meet their needs, which will help you meet yours. When you develop an ability to reflect on what's happening and can communicate effectively to remedy situations, achieve goals, and motivate people, you empower yourself and others, and you provide yourself with the space to grow as a leader.

What's Your EQ?

An IQ test rates an individual's cognitive intelligence quantitatively. It's a measurement that is universally accepted. There is, however, no universally accepted quantitative test to measure emotional intelligence. There are EQ instruments that attempt to assess emotional intelligence, but there isn't one universal standard. So, I've devised a simple self-assessment that can give you some insights into your emotional intelligence. I recommend taking this quiz to heighten your self-awareness before you read the rest of this chapter.

In the past, the "soft" skills that make a person emotionally intelligent were often overlooked in the workplace. These are skills related to understanding and managing people and relationships. Instead, technical and intellectual skills were emphasized. Now, experts in emotional intelligence claim that EQ is far more important than IQ in determining one's success at work. You have to know how to interact with and influence people to create success. You can have an IQ of 145, but if you don't know how to motivate people or know how to put a high-performing team together, you really don't have what it takes to make things happen. Leadership in today's highly connected world, where all kinds of people have to cooperate in order to achieve organizational goals, demands soft skills.

Emotional Intelligence Self-Assessment

Circle the answer that seems the most accurate.

1. **I can name my most important core values.**

never	rarely	sometimes	frequently	always
1	2	3	4	5

2. **I can name my greatest strengths and weaknesses.**

never	rarely	sometimes	frequently	always
1	2	3	4	5

3. **I am in control of my emotions.**

never	rarely	sometimes	frequently	always
1	2	3	4	5

4. **I understand what triggers me to lose control, and I know what to do to regain control when I lose it.**

never	rarely	sometimes	frequently	always
1	2	3	4	5

5. **I have an overall high degree of self-confidence.**

never	rarely	sometimes	frequently	always
1	2	3	4	5

6. **I treat myself with respect and take care of my physical and emotional needs.**

never	rarely	sometimes	frequently	always
1	2	3	4	5

7. **I treat other people with respect and fairness.**

never	rarely	sometimes	frequently	always
1	2	3	4	5

(continued)

Emotional Intelligence Self-Assessment
(continued)

8. I have sound moral principles and can be counted on to be honest and trustworthy.

never	rarely	sometimes	frequently	always
1	2	3	4	5

9. I'm a positive thinker and I see opportunities and possibilities.

never	rarely	sometimes	frequently	always
1	2	3	4	5

10. I know how to handle conflict and can see all sides of an issue as I work to solve problems.

never	rarely	sometimes	frequently	always
1	2	3	4	5

11. I am flexible and adapt quickly to new and changing situations.

never	rarely	sometimes	frequently	always
1	2	3	4	5

12. I trust my intuition and use it as a guide in decision making.

never	rarely	sometimes	frequently	always
1	2	3	4	5

13. I have empathy for people, understand their perspectives, and can react appropriately to their emotions.

never	rarely	sometimes	frequently	always
1	2	3	4	5

14. I believe that part of my success comes from helping others to develop, grow, and succeed.

never	rarely	sometimes	frequently	always
1	2	3	4	5

15. I empower others and don't feel that I need to have control or micromanage.

never	rarely	sometimes	frequently	always
1	2	3	4	5

16. I am adept at building teams and bringing diverse people together in support of mutual goals.

never	rarely	sometimes	frequently	always
1	2	3	4	5

(continued)

Emotional Intelligence Self-Assessment
(concluded)

17. I build consensus and collaborate well.

never	rarely	sometimes	frequently	always
1	2	3	4	5

18. I have faith in my ability to make sound judgments and good decisions.

never	rarely	sometimes	frequently	always
1	2	3	4	5

19. I'm successful at building relationships.

never	rarely	sometimes	frequently	always
1	2	3	4	5

20. I coach and mentor others.

never	rarely	sometimes	frequently	always
1	2	3	4	5

21. I have the ability to influence and motivate people.

never	rarely	sometimes	frequently	always
1	2	3	4	5

22. I have clear boundaries and know what I want and need.

never	rarely	sometimes	frequently	always
1	2	3	4	5

23. I am a good listener who can hear below the surface of the conversation.

never	rarely	sometimes	frequently	always
1	2	3	4	5

24. I give feedback that is immediate, open, direct, caring, and honest.

never	rarely	sometimes	frequently	always
1	2	3	4	5

25. I know how to ask the right questions, and don't feel that I have to have all the right answers.

never	rarely	sometimes	frequently	always
1	2	3	4	5

Add up your scores to get your overall EQ rating: 25 or under is poor; 26 to 50 is fair; 51 to 75 is good; 76 to 100 is very good; 101 to 125 is excellent.

Develop Trust through Good Judgment

If you want to be an integrated leader whom people *want* to follow, you need to build trust. People need to feel confident that you'll make the right decisions, to feel safe communicating with you, and to trust that you are looking out for their best interests as well as for the interests of the organization. One of the most disheartening situations we can be in is to work for a boss whom we can't trust to look out for us or to make sound decisions.

Your organization and your team should come first. If you want people to follow you and you want to motivate them to meet their goals, they need to believe that what you are advocating is beneficial for the organization and for them and not solely for your own benefit. Team members and peers don't want to feel that they are simply putting feathers in *your* cap or helping *you* to climb ladders. They need to know that *they'll* benefit from their efforts, and they must feel that what you are asking them to do makes good business sense.

If you are continually making mistakes or making decisions that backfire, direct reports and others will lose their desire to follow you. You're being paid to use your intelligence to make decisions that produce successful results. As a leader, you have more formal power than your team members and you probably make more money, but if they believe they can make better decisions than you, they will resent your lack of good judgment. Not only will you lose credibility and respect, but they will end up losing hope and feel demotivated. You build trust by putting the good of the organization and your team ahead of your own ego needs, and by basing every decision on sound judgment. Do you have all the facts? Does your rationale make sense? Do you believe in your own decision?

Confidence in Confidentiality

A true leader earns the trust of others. Can people come to you with issues and problems and know that you will hold whatever they tell you in confidence? If you are unable to hold a confidence, it is usually a sign that you put your needs above theirs. One of the worst things that can happen to a team is for the leader to be a blabbermouth and the instigator of gossip. Loose lips sink ships. As a leader, it's your responsibility to know what can be shared, whom it can be shared with, and when to talk about certain issues. If people believe you can't be trusted to hold their confidences, they will withhold important information about what's really happening, which can skew your perspective.

Moreover, rather than getting your team to focus on best practices, your indiscretions will eventually pit people against each other as they listen to what you say about different team members. So, build trust by keeping confidences and by understanding the fine line about what is appropriate and what is not appropriate to disclose.

Leadership Links with Learning

Integrated leadership develops from learning and from building competencies in each of the domains of self, others, and work. Integrated, emotionally intelligent leaders are open and positive, flexible and adaptable. They allow themselves to be vulnerable: to seek help when they need it and to admit what they don't know.

You won't develop your emotional intelligence if you remain closed to new ideas or are afraid of admitting your own lack of knowledge. There is a fluidity in leadership that comes from being able to move between knowing and not knowing, between being an expert and being a learner. Although you need good judgment, you must let go of being judgmental, righteous, and rigid. Instead, respect and interact with people who are different from you and who have flaws, fears, and hidden emotional needs, just as you do.

Leaders who are emotionally intelligent are also able to see the complexity of the world. Rather than being "black and white" thinkers, they see the shades of gray that enshroud relationships and situations. Instead of rigidly adhering to a belief, they have the emotional strength and dexterity to examine beliefs, the courage to challenge their own convictions, and the flexibility to bend enough to see the world through the other person's eyes.

Emotionally intelligent people don't necessarily like everyone they meet; they simply are able to listen actively to another point of view in order to understand how to respond appropriately. They are able to look at a situation objectively and can make rational decisions with self-confidence and assurance. People with good EQ can disapprove of another person's decisions or behavior and still treat that person with dignity and respect. The lesson here is that you can learn win/win ways in which to interact or work together even when you don't like or don't agree with the other person.

EQ Bridges Differences

It is only human to like certain people more than others. Generally, the people we like have behavioral styles or interests similar to our own or that mesh with our style in some beneficial way. But it's important to recognize that a variety of styles are needed at work in order to create a balanced and diversified approach to problems and issues. As a leader, it's critical for you to be aware of and manage your own prejudices or biases. You don't have to like everyone equally, but you do have to treat everyone with respect and set standards that apply equally to everyone.

Read the case study on the next page and determine how you would have handled the situation. At first glance, the case of Lyn and Tony seems to be strictly a case of gender differences. However, it's really much more than that: It's also a case of true diversity in style and culture. Often our differences stem from more than just one layer of our personality.

People who are emotionally intelligent don't feel that they have to back down or cave in around their values in order to appease someone else, but they do know where and how to be appropriately flexible. They understand themselves and can confidently operate with high standards and integrity. Able to stay rooted in their own authenticity, they can compromise with others without compromising their own principles. Operating with self-awareness, self-control, and clear boundaries, they don't allow themselves to become embroiled in dysfunctional situations and can deal assertively with disruptive, unprofessional, or unethical behavior.

EQ and Relational Competence

Researchers at the Stone Center at Wellesley College, interested in the psychology of women and the subject of women's leadership, have been building a body of work known as "relational cultural theory." Joyce Fletcher, one of the Center's researchers, describes the basic tenets of this theory in her book *Disappearing Acts*. She says that growth comes from interactions in which there is "mutual empathy and mutual empowerment." In order to develop relationally, she believes that people need the strengths of "empathy, vulnerability, the ability to experience and express emotion,

Diversity: The Case of Lyn and Tony

Lyn is from an Asian culture and a religious background that is strongly rooted in traditions of right and wrong. She believes that some behaviors are correct and others are not. Lyn is having a particularly tough time dealing with Tony, one of the star performers on her team. Some of her objections to Tony's behaviors are valid—he is loud, and he swears and drinks too much. An extrovert, Tony talks a lot, is out for a good time, and doesn't like to pay attention to details. Tony is all about having fun—he just wants to make the sales and bring in the big bucks.

Lyn, on the other hand, is a soft-spoken introvert who focuses on details and procedures, which is a strength in her role. Her natural style is to focus on business and keep the personal and the professional separate. She isn't comfortable hobnobbing with the guys at the bar after work.

Lyn's distrust and dislike for Tony is so intense that she can't find a way to focus on any of his attributes: He is charming and funny, and underneath his rough-edge demeanor, he really just wants to be liked. Tony doesn't know what to do with the fact that Lyn can't stand him, so, he lashes out at her more, making fun of her and finding ways to undermine her. This has fed into the negative cycle between them.

Their problems reflect style differences, gender differences (Lyn is the only woman in the group), and cultural differences. Although she outranks Tony on the organizational chart, he is well positioned and brings in lots of money. People (meaning men) are beginning to take sides and are lining up behind the guy with a smile on his face. Tony is happy-go-lucky; Lyn is serious and withdrawn. Tony knows how to build relationships to advance himself, and Lyn doesn't. Nevertheless, Lyn is far more intelligent than Tony in the hard skills of running the business, but seems averse to appeasing him. In his presence, her body language shows her disdain, which then triggers him to act out in a manner that stirs her disapproval even more. They are in a negative dance together.

If you were the leader of this team, what would you do?

the ability to participate in the development of another, and an expectation that relational interactions can yield mutual growth."

I believe this concept of mutual empathy, mutual empowerment, and growth through relational interactions is similar to emotional intelligence. I use the phrase *relational competence* to refer to a leader's understanding that her success and power come out of her ability to help others grow and flourish. Leaders who possess relational competence as well as emotional intelligence integrate their vision and their strategic thinking with their ability to empower others. These leaders cooperate and collaborate; they work together toward shared goals, and operate with high degrees of trust, respect, and commitment. Rather than needing to develop and gratify their own individual egos, leaders who are relationally competent succeed by developing *team* egos.

One of the best examples of relational competence that I have come across is a job-sharing team of two vice presidents at Verizon. For over a dozen years, these two women climbed the ladder together. When they first proposed their job-sharing strategy as middle managers in the late '80s, they were told that two women working together would never be able to manage well and that their opportunity to share one job was an experiment likely to fail. They have climbed up the corporate ladder together—rung by rung—because of their ability to share power and grow *together*. These two women have ultimate trust in each other and must collaborate on every aspect of their job. They are true partners, depending on each other for their success, and their performance depends on the quality of their interactions. Mutual growth and development is a requisite for achieving their goals. Their ability to read each other and respond to each other with caring, honesty, and candor has enabled them to carve out ground-breaking careers and forge lives that meet their shared values of excellence and balance. They are truly integrated leaders.

Leadership and Parenting: The Same Skill Set

People who demonstrate relational competence are concerned about their own growth and success, but they go one step further: They actually gauge their success by the growth of others. When talking about the relational competence and emotional intelligence critical to integrated leadership, I often use the metaphor of "parenting." Effective parenting means nurturing your children, setting boundaries, giving them guidance and support, clarifying expectations and responsibilities, allowing them to make mistakes, and holding them accountable. Your "success" as a parent is determined by your ability to help your kids grow into emotionally well-adjusted, responsible, productive, loving adults.

Your success as a leader in the business world is similarly linked to your ability to help your staff and employees develop into satisfied, motivated, responsible, productive performers. When you operate with relational competence and emotional intelligence, you offer guidance and support and contribute to the growth and development of others. Your power comes not from being "over" others, but from being "with" them in their development. You believe that their needs are more important than yours. This is what some leadership experts call "servant leadership"—you serve the needs of followers (the people who depend on you). I see leadership more as the ability to integrate followers' needs in a deeply connected way with your own needs: They need you and you need them. As the leader, you are responsible for their well-being and development. Their success reflects your success. You wouldn't be successful without them, and they wouldn't be successful without you.

Integrated Leadership: Accessing Masculine and Feminine Energy

Integrated leaders are flexible and adaptable, and can assess situations and respond appropriately by adjusting their leadership style, moving from one style to another depending on what's needed in the moment. In the last decade, there has been a lot of discussion about women's leadership styles and whether or not they are different from men's. Research on women's leadership suggests that women do tend to differ from men in the way they approach leadership. This does *not* mean, however, that all women lead one way and that all men lead another way.

In distinguishing leadership styles, I speak about one style as "command and control" and the other as "relational and empowering." I think of the command and control style as having more masculine energy and the relational and empowering style as having more feminine energy. The masculine approach is more linear, more objective, more focused, more competitive, and more action-oriented, and communication is generally top-down. The feminine approach is more holistic, more subjective, more connected, more collaborative, more process oriented, and communication is usually two-way.

Real power and success comes from integrating the two and being able to access both masculine and feminine energy at any given time:

■ The leader who knows when to process and when to act, and when to be directive and when to be collaborative, will be more successful.

■ The leader who appreciates the value of the big picture but who knows how to focus on the task at hand or knows how to prioritize will be more effective.

■ The leader who knows that facts are critical for analyzing situations, but always pays attention to his or her intuition, will be the leader who makes better decisions.

Leadership Styles Determine Organizational Culture

The culture of an organization reflects the style of its leaders. I've seen some organizations led by people who were so relational they couldn't make hard decisions or muster the authority they needed to lead effectively. The leaders weren't able to stay focused on their vision and inspire and motivate people. They didn't have the courage to take responsibility for making tough decisions. Trying to please everyone, they pleased no one. The leaders didn't trust themselves to make good decisions.

I've observed other companies where people didn't feel free to raise questions or disagree. Managers were afraid to voice their real concerns. To be a good team player meant one had to constantly agree and comply, even if it meant carrying out activities that didn't make sense or were doomed to fail. The leaders really didn't want to hear opposing views—they wanted to be in command and didn't trust their people to make good decisions.

An integrated leader combines the best of both styles. Depending on the situation, integrating both styles allows the leader to be competitive yet collaborative, and to know when to direct and when to coach. The integrated leader can see the whole picture as well as all the pieces of a situation, and can be rational and objective, yet operate intuitively. An integrated style balances action with reflection, and is both a top-down and bottom-up process.

Look at the leadership chart below and see if you can determine which style best represents you. Do you lean to one style more than to the other? Or are you a combination of both? If you lean too much on one side, think about situations when it might be helpful for you to shift over to the other leadership style. Think about your answer and any resistance you might have. What's causing you to resist? Notice the beliefs that you have around each style. What do your answers reveal about your leadership?

Leadership Styles	
Command and Control (masculine energy)	**Relational and Empowering (feminine energy)**
■ Authoritarian, paternalistic ■ Competitive, win/lose mentality ■ Has compartmentalized thinking, focuses awareness ■ Rational, linear, objective ■ Exclusive, hierarchical ■ Top-down communicator ■ Action-Oriented	■ Coaches, mentors ■ Collaborative, builds consensus ■ Sees the whole picture, makes connections ■ Intuitive, holistic, subjective ■ Inclusive, shares power ■ Two-way communicator ■ Process-Oriented

Integrating Styles: The Story of Mike

If you cannot easily switch styles or combine the two, your leadership effectiveness will be jeopardized. The story of Mike, a former client, demonstrates this point. Mike is an alpha male kind of guy, with lots of masculine energy and presence. He is physically big, smart, and highly proficient technically; his skill and physical presence command respect. He isn't afraid to yell at people when he is mad at them or when they aren't performing as they should, or to strut his presence to get his team to pay attention. Mike is an action, not a process person, who doesn't always control his emotions.

Mike's style worked well for him until he found himself in a new organization due to a restructuring. The new organizational culture and his new boss focused more on a collaborative approach. Mike's leadership style of commanding others by barking orders wasn't as effective in his new position. From his previous experiences, he had learned to lead with an authoritarian, directive approach. When people didn't perform up to par or didn't demonstrate sufficient expertise or commitment, he often lost respect for them and lost control over his temper. People had made demands and screamed at him in the past and he had accepted it, so it didn't occur to him that there were other ways to lead. In this particular environment, however, his leadership style was actually causing him to lose credibility as a leader, but he didn't find it easy to move into a different style.

More and more research is being conducted on the brain and how it shapes the way in which we approach the world. There is a difference between the brains of men and women. Some of this research indicates that certain people are naturally more inclined to being empathic than others, but this doesn't mean that new behaviors and ways of interacting with others can't be learned. However, learning takes time and the first step in the learning process is self-awareness. We need to first discover what it is we need to learn.

Once Mike became aware of what needed to shift in this style and approach, he could focus on making those changes. He had to let go of his belief that leadership is only about commanding and learn how to empathize with others and communicate in ways that were at first extremely uncomfortable for him. Rather than losing his temper with team members who were not performing well, Mike worked on managing his anger and listening on deeper levels so that he could learn ways to support them in their development. He practiced new communication techniques that enabled him to discover what people needed and how he could help them. This kind of learning, however, calls for practice and takes time. Mike didn't change overnight, but today he is a leader who knows how to be both directive and collaborative.

Dealing with People You Don't Respect

Many high-performing individuals have problems dealing with people they don't respect. This can really hang people up and get them stuck. If you find that you have this problem and just don't want to deal with people for whom you have little respect, here's an analogy to think about: Imagine that you are a world leader who must deal with the leaders of other countries. You don't respect a couple of these leaders—in fact, you don't trust them and you don't like them. Do you take an all-or-nothing approach? Or do you try to meet them somewhere in the middle? Do you keep them at a distance, or do you try to get them on your side through influence and persuasion? To influence and persuade, you need to understand what they want and what they need to hear, and shape your language and communication in a way that enables them to respond. This isn't easy, and it's certainly not always successful. Their response might be erratic—one time your persuasive strategy might work, and another time it might not. But do you give up? You might feel that you shouldn't need to persuade or influence them since you feel you're in the right, but if you give up or don't bother to understand their beliefs, wants, and needs, it might mean all-out war. In war, everybody loses something.

The Problem with Delegating Perfection

People who are emotionally intelligent realize that perfection doesn't exist. In the workplace, integrated leaders understand that everyone makes mistakes. They are results-oriented and strive toward high-quality outcomes, but they don't get hung up in perfectionism or in the arrogance of believing they are always right. Integrated leaders have a degree of humility about them, are open to different ways of achieving results, and understand that problems can be solved in a variety of ways. They also appreciate diverse perspectives; managers who demand that things be done their way and can't keep their hands off the work of their teams break down trust and demotivate and disempower others. Aside from the negative impacts of micromanagement, "controlling" bosses rob themselves of the time they need to develop their own higher level skills.

Ask yourself what you need to do to let go and trust others to do their work. The more you can empower your team to accept responsibility for their outcomes and solve their own problems, the more effective your team will be—and the more you will develop your leadership potential and the leadership skills of your team members.

If you're a manager mired in the tactical and fail to take the time to think and plan strategically, you probably need to be delegating more. This ability to relinquish some control to others seems to be a typical passage or transitional stage that managers must go through on their way to becoming good leaders. Delegating can be one of the hardest leadership skills to learn, because it requires faith and trust that your people might indeed make mistakes, but they won't utterly fail. In this way, leadership once again resembles parenting: As a parent, it's your job to develop your children and help them learn and grow. For the most part, their behavior reflects your parenting skills. As a leader, the quality of your team reflects your ability to develop its members. If they aren't where they should be, it's ultimately your responsibility. If they don't have the necessary skills to do their jobs, you need to ask yourself: *"What haven't I been doing that I should have been doing?"* It's *your* job to set expectations, assess their skill sets, and help them develop—not only so that they can do their jobs and meet their goals, but also to support them as they grow professionally.

If you have done what was needed to support their growth and development and they still aren't where they should be, then you need to make one of the more difficult decisions of leadership, which is to let people go. If someone is not pulling his weight, you do your team, your organization, and yourself a disservice by allowing him to hang on. Perhaps this person is not suited for the particular job he is in: If that is the case, it's your responsibility as the leader to remedy this by getting him into a more suitable position in which he *can* make a contribution. If he still can't perform, it's your responsibility to let him go.

Emotional Intelligence Summary Steps

Over the past several years, the entire world has been impacted by the behaviors of corporate and political leaders who failed to understand others or consider the impact and consequences of their actions on others. They neglected their responsibility to their people and their organizations and demonstrated a lack of respect for the values they were supposed to be upholding. These leaders were anything but emotionally intelligent.

When you lead with emotional intelligence, you have the ability to build a bridge between yourself and others. If you want to improve your EQ, you must identify your emotional triggers and know how to control your emotions appropriately. You must recognize your own biases, and learn how to understand the perspectives of others—even when you differ or disagree. Without this understanding of emotions and how they can be managed, you won't be able to communicate effectively. And if you can't communicate effectively, you won't be able to influence people, build relationships, and form alliances that are critical to your success.

Use the self-assessment provided earlier in the chapter to determine the areas of emotional intelligence in which you shine, and the areas that need to be developed. Decide where your weaknesses are and develop some smart quarterly goals for yourself to strengthen them. Determine your leadership style and make sure you know how to combine styles or switch back and forth between styles. By constantly honing your EQ, you will gradually become a truly integrated leader who operates from a place of grounded self-confidence and self-control—a leader who can be counted on to make good judgments, even in stressful or chaotic times.

Coaching Questions on Emotional Intelligence

Answer the following questions, reflecting on what you need to be more emotionally intelligent.

How emotionally intelligent are you?

What aspects of emotional intelligence do you need to develop?

What are your "hot buttons"? What triggers your emotions the most?

What techniques can you use to gain better control over your emotional response?

How humble are you? In what ways do you demonstrate that your team and your organization come first?

Assess your decision-making ability and the accuracy of your judgments. What's preventing you from making better judgments and decisions?

(continued)

Coaching Questions on
Emotional Intelligence *(concluded)*

How good are you at understanding style differences? How can you improve your ability to empathize with others?

How good are you at using different styles of leadership? What do you need to do to be more flexible?

What influences and motivates the people you interact with? How can you improve your influencing and motivating skills?

How approachable are you? How often do your peers, direct reports, and your boss talk openly and candidly to you?

How much do others trust you? What do you need to do to foster greater trust and respect?

How good are you at delegating and empowering others? What can you do to improve in these areas?

What are your ethical boundaries?

CHAPTER FOUR

Be Assertive: Know How to Communicate Effectively

Almost every writer on leadership issues emphasizes how important it is for leaders to be effective communicators. I believe effective communicators are people who know how to be assertive—in every aspect of their communication, they express their thoughts, beliefs, and feelings in honest, direct, and appropriate ways. Their ability to communicate assertively flows from their emotional intelligence.

Leaders who are assertive communicators are comfortable with themselves and project a confident image. They use good body language and know how to engage people by making eye contact without getting in the other person's face. They are interested in others, ask questions, and actively listen in order to deepen their understanding. They also have the self-confidence to advocate for themselves and to make clear, direct requests. In addition, assertive communicators have clear boundaries—they won't be taken advantage of, and they won't take advantage of others. Assertive communicators know how to disagree without being disagreeable. They don't allow themselves to get off balance and act out, and they don't get pulled into dysfunctional or destructive conversations.

Assertiveness is about giving and getting respect. Bottom line, assertive communicators respect themselves and others and communicate in a way that opens up space for understanding and connection.

Assertive versus Aggressive

Some people confuse assertiveness with being confrontational and aggressive. Being a leader in their minds means being tough enough to bark out orders and not back down. This can be confusing to women who are told that they must be aggressive if they want to make it in business. The women who take that advice can get labeled with the "B" word, and end up offending everyone—doing themselves great harm in the process. Sometimes men mistake aggression for assertiveness; confrontational, aggressive behavior to them demonstrates their virility and power. "Aggressive" communication, however, is negative, because it lacks the key element of respect for others. Whether male or female, aggressive people are out to win their points and prove they're right, regardless of the cost to others.

Aggressive communication is confrontational and attacking. It has a competitive win/lose feel to it, because the aggressive person wants to get his or her way or prove a point. Aggressiveness can show up in the form of screaming and cursing, but it also manifests itself when someone who might not be loud makes demands on others and backs them into corners. When you are asked to do something that you don't think is ethically right or the correct thing to do, and you are being pressured to do it to serve the purpose of the person pressuring you, you are encountering aggressive behavior. As an integrated leader, your job is to make sure that you provide the space for people to feel respected and heard, and to create an environment that reinforces ethical behavior.

Passive Communicators: The Retreaters

Another non-assertive style is passive communication. People communicating passively avoid confrontation and conflict at all cost. With passiveness there is a lack of respect of the self: The passive person doesn't have enough self-confidence to make his thoughts and feelings known. Passive communicators go along with others and comply with requests, without making requests of their own. Rather than figuring out what other people want or need and how to communicate about those wants and needs, the passive person remains silent and retreats. Extremely passive people aren't effective leaders, because they never seem to have an opinion or take a stand. They can't be relied on in a crunch because it's not evident that they'll take a risk or have the courage to speak out.

In order to be a leader, you need to be consistent and tell your followers what you value, where you're going, and why you're going there. It's your responsibility to address difficult issues and integrate different points of view. It's also your responsibility to take a stand and make difficult decisions, whether they're popular or not.

Passive-Aggressive Communicators: The Alienators

Passive-aggressive communicators also lack assertiveness. Each of us knows at least one person who communicates passive-aggressively, and we all get frustrated dealing with this style of communication. And each of us has at some point probably been guilty of passive-aggressive communication ourselves. When people communicate passive aggressively, there is an appearance of agreement on the surface, but their veiled words contain a hidden agenda—passive-aggressive communicators say one thing, yet mean something else. For one reason or another, the person who communicates passive aggressively finds it either too difficult to communicate directly or is too devious to be open and honest.

Some people who communicate passive aggressively operate out of a belief that they need to protect the feelings of others: They feel that the truth might hurt. They project their own insecurities on others, without respecting the ability of other people to handle honest, respectful, appropriate communication. And some passive-aggressive communicators are narcissistic or arrogant. They couch what they say not out of a desire to protect the person they're communicating with, but in order to somehow get an upper hand without looking as though they are. Some will subtly try to stab people in the back or deliberately confuse them in order to fulfill their own agenda. In either case, passive aggressiveness causes confusion.

Whether or not they mean harm, people who demonstrate a consistent style of passive-aggressive communication break down trust. Because issues aren't dealt with directly, they get pushed underground, which sets the stage for gossip and sabotage. A manager who can't make direct requests and provide clear expectations creates confusion and chaos, which leads to anger and resentment and paves the way for errors and poor performance. A boss who tells his team one thing and then says something else behind the team's back creates a culture of distrust. Over time, team members become demotivated and won't go the extra mile.

Another form of passive-aggressive communication occurs when people portray themselves as the "victim" and blame whatever goes wrong on someone else. When managers don't own their own mistakes, they create an environment of fear, because no one is sure who will get blamed. Moreover, team members lose confidence, because it's hard to look up to a "victim." A leader takes responsibility and owns results—good or bad.

A manager who communicates passive aggressively is likely to lack self-respect and not respect others enough to be open with them. It's a lose/lose style, because the truth never emerges. If issues and problems aren't dealt with honestly, they won't get successfully resolved. The leader's role is to bring people together to achieve results, not to be an obstacle.

Communication Styles	
Assertive Style	Respect for self and others; express thoughts, beliefs, and feelings in honest, direct, appropriate ways, win/win
Aggressive Style	Lack of respect for others; offensive attack, confront in ways that create defensiveness, win/lose
Passive Style	Lack of respect for self; retreat, withdraw, lose/win
Passive-Aggressive Style	Lack of respect for self and others; veiled, hidden agendas, resentment, sabotage, lose/lose

Staying Grounded and Assertive

Your psychological perspective and behavioral style can affect the way in which you communicate with others. If you are the type of person who focuses on pleasing others or you have extreme discomfort with disagreement, you might passively retreat or send passive-aggressive mixed messages, without meaning to and without even realizing that you are doing it. If you aren't feeling grounded (if you don't feel that you have your emotions under control and can communicate in a rational and calm manner), you might vacillate between aggressiveness, passiveness, and passive aggressiveness, causing fear and confusion. People won't know what to expect from you and will probably avoid you rather than risk getting attacked or having to spend emotional energy trying to figure out your agenda or what's going on with you. As a leader, you need people coming *to* you—not running away from you.

All three people in the case study on the following page failed to communicate assertively, which fed into their inability to manage their business situation properly. When people fail to communicate assertively, it can create or exacerbate a problem. The atmosphere can also become hostile, draining people's energy and inhibiting their ability to operate productively and efficiently. Each person has a responsibility to communicate assertively. After reading the case study, determine how each of the individuals could have been a more assertive communicator. Answer the following questions: What communication styles are each of the players using in this case? How are the styles they are using hindering their abilities to lead? What should they have done to communicate assertively?

Presence: An Essential Intangible of Leadership

Presence can be hard to describe, but you know when someone has it and when someone doesn't. In the dictionary, presence is defined as "bearing, personality or appearance that is characterized by poise and confidence." But it also is defined as having "a supernatural or divine spirit to it." I think of presence as a combination of an appealing physical appearance, confident body language, assertive communication skills, and positive engaging

Non-Assertive Communication: The Case of Sonia and Diana

Sonia, an extremely attractive woman in her early 30s, is the HR manager of a growing multinational firm that recently went through a merger. She climbed the corporate ladder fairly quickly and is now responsible for a global team that operates out of four countries. In the latest merger, Sonia was in charge of managing the integration process. She had to work closely with Diana, an HR peer from the other company. Diana, in her late 40s, is located in a different country.

As is typical, there is some redundancy as a result of a merger, so Sonia and Diana must work together to determine which people from each company will be filling certain key roles; however, Sonia has the final say. Unfortunately, Diana took an immediate dislike to Sonia, thinking that she was too young to take on such an important role. Her responses to Sonia were snide and condescending. Sensing Diana's resistance, Sonia tried to reach out, but she was rebuffed. She in turn developed an intense dislike for Diana. The interaction between the two women grew extremely tense and hostile.

Diana made underhanded remarks in front of Sonia and behind her back, and tried to undermine Sonia whenever she could. Sonia, who has a volatile temper, was trying hard to control it; rather than letting her anger loose, she decided that the best way to deal with Diana was to avoid her. Since they worked about a thousand miles apart, this was fairly easy to do, and Sonia kept communication to a minimum.

During that time, Sonia made the decision to put someone from her own company in a key role, instead of someone from Diana's, which infuriated Diana. In retaliation, Diana contacted Sonia's boss, Dick, to complain about Sonia's performance. Dick is a hands-off manager who doesn't like conflict and didn't want to deal with the two women himself. He told Diana to put her complaints in writing, but this escalated the issue to a formal status. When Sonia discovered what had happened, she completely lost her temper and lambasted Dick for not defending her. Sonia wanted to contact Diana and address the whole issue, but Dick, afraid of a blow-up, instructed her to stay away from Diana for the time being.

energy, which actually creates some kind of magnetic field around a person that attracts others. When a person has all these traits, they have an aura of power that translates into the presence of a leader.

An appealing physical appearance doesn't mean that you have to have movie-star looks or spend a fortune on clothes, but it does mean that you need to dress professionally and appropriately. Your appearance sends a message about who you are. You might not be able to judge a book by its cover, but, whether you like it or not, people will judge you by what you look like.

Your body language contributes to your presence, because it communicates more about you than anything you say. It reveals your level of confidence and to some degree your emotional intelligence. Good body language demonstrates your openness to others, your willingness to listen, your understanding of others, and the issues at hand. To project the presence of a leader, it's critical for you to know how to control your body and teach it to speak the language of leadership.

To be a consistent assertive communicator, the 3 Vs (verbal, vocal, and visual) of communication need to be aligned. Verbal communication refers to the actual words that you use. Vocal communication represents the tone of your voice, and visual comprises all your nonverbal behaviors.

Women often complain that their voices aren't heard and their ideas are grabbed by men. I've watched women in my workshops share their experiences and even as they tell their stories, their body language demonstrates their lack of assertiveness. Their bodies shrink or collapse in some way and their voices get softer. They do not exude the presence of leadership.

Your Communication Style

Think about your usual style of communication, and answer the following questions:

Which non-assertive communication style do you revert to when you are not feeling confident or don't have your emotions under control (aggressive, passive, or passive aggressive)?

What keeps you from communicating in an assertive style? Who or what triggers you to communicate non-assertively?

What beliefs do you hold that keep you from being assertive? (Cultures and families have beliefs that influence the way we communicate—for example, the belief that women should defer to men or that it's not polite to be direct.)

What fears keep you from being assertive?

What behaviors do you need to change in order to be more assertive?

If you want to be heard and you want to be acknowledged for your ideas, you must demonstrate confidence. Project your voice so that it lands where you want it to land with the resonance you want it to have. "Own" your ideas by making it clear that you are connected to them. Don't retreat, and don't attack. But think on your feet.

A certain amount of energy is transmitted through body language: People can see whether you are positive or negative, whether you are charged and full of energy or whether your battery is low. For the most part, energy is the spiritual (beyond the physical) aspect of communication. The energy of presence comes from within a person and emanates outward, engaging and embracing others. As I already mentioned, on a quantum level, we are masses of energy. Even our thoughts are energetic and influence not only our own body, but that energy—both negative and positive—moves out beyond us to influence others. The positive energy of a leader contains passion, vision, and hope. Others can feel it without actually touching it. It's not always visible and accessible through our five senses; yet we know it's there. Some people call this charisma.

To develop your presence as a leader, pay attention to every aspect of your communication. What message does your physical appearance transmit? Are you being assertive in your communications? What kinds of words do you use? What is the tone of your voice? What does your body language say? What kind of energy do you exude?

Observe your communication patterns so that you can make necessary corrections. When positive energy is combined with assertive communication skills, good body language, and an appealing personal attitude and appearance, the result is *presence*.

Listening Skills for Leaders

Listening skills are critical to communication, and they are a key component in being assertive. If we can't "hear" what other people are saying—that is, if we don't get what they mean—we can easily misunderstand them. If we misunderstand others, we won't respond properly. Think about all the miscommunication that goes on everyday in the workplace. As a leader, it's your job to make sure that you actively listen on a deep level to those around you in order to have a good understanding of what people want and need so that you can properly guide them. Active listening is a key skill required for leading, mentoring, and coaching.

Each of us listens in particular ways. Shaped by our experiences and our psyche, we hear what we have been conditioned to listen for. Therefore, we have a tendency to respond to people, ask questions, and shape our conversations based on what we're hearing, as opposed to what others are intending us to hear. Without realizing we are doing it, we filter information. We create meaning based on our own experiences and interpretations of the world. For instance, if you are a person with the tendency to view your glass as half empty rather than half full, you're more likely to hear the negative side of people's stories and listen for the bad news.

When you only hear a biased version of events, your view of reality is skewed. If you have developed good communication skills, you can strip away your own meanings and interpretations and listen openly to others without judging them. You need to be aware of your own biases so that you can practice active listening; this means that you will try to understand what others are saying without projecting your own interpretations and meanings on them. When you listen actively, you can hear below the level of others' words to understand how what they're saying affects them.

One way to become more adept at deep listening is to talk less. If you're doing all the talking, you can't possibly be listening. Practice silence: Hold back and let others speak.

To understand what other barriers might impact your ability to listen on deep levels, look at the list on the next two pages, adapted from *Messages: The Communication Skills Book* by Matthew McKay, Martha Davis, and Patrick Fanning. Check off the barriers that apply to you. Are there one or two that are particularly troublesome for you or can you relate to a majority of them?

My Listening Barriers

You can begin to improve your listening skills by paying attention to what happens when you communicate and by identifying patterns that get in the way of listening on a deep level. Here's an example: My major listening block is comparing. When people tell me something that is of particular interest to me—something that I wish I had done or experienced—I have a tendency to start comparing myself to them. My envy button gets pushed: I start wishing I could have figured out a way to have the experience myself, or I start thinking of ways I can make it happen for me. I'm not focused on them; I'm focused on me.

As you become more aware of your own biases and barriers, red flags will begin flying to alert you when you are not listening deeply. Then you can shift your attention and refocus on what is being said. The key to being a deep, active listener is to remain open, nonjudgmental, and focused on the other person. When you listen deeply, you empower yourself because you open up space to hear possibilities and to deepen understanding and learning. You also empower

others, because when people truly feel heard and understood, they are more open to listening and learning
themselves.

Listening Barriers Exercise

Check off the barriers that tend to interfere with *your* listening the
most. How many barriers keep you from being the active listener
that you would like to be?

_____   **Advising:** After hearing only a few words, you believe that
you know how to solve the person's problem and you start
offering advice.

_____   **Comparing:** As you listen to the other person, your
insecurities get triggered, and you start comparing yourself to
the person—assessing which one of you is better, more
knowledgeable, more competent, etc.

_____   **Daydreaming:** You get triggered by something the other
person says and you're off in your own world. You don't
have a clue what the person said to you.

_____   **Derailing:** You find the subject matter uncomfortable, so you
abruptly change the subject or interrupt with a joke.

_____   **Filling-in:** You don't let the other person finish her sentence;
instead you finish it for her.

_____   **Filtering:** You only listen to the part of the message that is
important to you, and tune out the rest. You either pay
attention to things that might be emotionally threatening (and
fail to hear anything good), or you only hear what is good
(and fail to hear the parts that are negative).

(continued)

Listening Barriers Exercise *(concluded)*

_____ **Identifying:** You identify with what the person is telling you and swing the conversation back to yourself, telling how something similar happened to you. You become engrossed in telling *your* story, and don't really listen to the other person or allow her the space to continue her story.

_____ **Judging:** You make hasty judgments about people before completely listening to what they have to say.

_____ **Mind Reading:** You look for what you perceive to be the truth, and end up making assumptions that have little to do with what the person is actually saying to you.

_____ **Placating:** You want to be nice and supportive; therefore, you voice agreement with everything that is being said, even if you don't really agree. Because you don't really want to disagree, you don't listen deeply enough to fully examine the other person's viewpoint.

_____ **Rehearsing:** Rather than listening, you are mentally preparing what you are going to say. You might *look* interested, but you're really concentrating on planning how you're going to respond.

_____ **Sparring:** You quickly disagree with the other person because you have a strong point of view. The other person feels like she hasn't had a chance to be heard.

The listening barriers of others can also affect your ability to communicate effectively. For example, as I said in Chapter One, one of my core values is having my voice heard. I can get triggered when I'm in a conversation with an "identifier" who steals my air space. I feel that I'm just starting to tell *my* story, and all of a sudden the dynamics change and the other person is telling me *hers*. I then feel that I have to listen to her, so my buttons get pushed and I start to shut down. And as I shut down, I get aggravated, yet I don't fight for the air space. I just shut down. Our conversation becomes negatively affected, and the other person probably doesn't even realize it. The conversation loses the potential benefit it might have had.

So, become aware of your barriers and the barriers of others that are likely to trigger you. Notice what you do and devise and test ways to refocus yourself. Then practice, practice, practice staying "present" in your conversations.

Listening: A Key to Influencing

In most of today's companies, the emphasis is on flattening the organization and placing leaders at every level. Leaders in flattened organizations must be able to get people to work toward goals without anyone holding formal authority. This calls for influencing, and you can't influence people if you don't know how to communicate effectively with them. The more accurately you hear others, the more you understand their viewpoints, their interpretation of events, and the way they make meaning out of situations. The more you understand their thinking, the greater ability you'll have to recognize how they listen. The more you understand about their listening, the greater ability you'll have to shape your own message so that you will be understood. When you are correctly heard, and when you correctly hear others, you gain the chance to influence them, which is what leadership is about—influencing others to achieve goals.

There are a variety of styles and strategies for influencing. You can work collaboratively toward common goals and energize people so that they're excited about achieving goals. Or you can clarify people's thinking and leverage your own expertise. Or you can sell people on the benefits of goals and compromise through an exchange process. All of these styles and strategies, however, require you to understand what people need, value, and want, as well as to recognize what motivates and inspires them. One time it might be a hard direct sell, and another time it might be a negotiated compromise. In one situation, you might need to be inspirational, and in another, you might have to be logical and rational. But you won't understand how to influence without listening.

If you can determine people's behavioral style by listening to them and observing them, you can shape your message so that they can hear you better. People with different behavioral styles have different listening tendencies. What follows is a *very, very* brief summary of behavioral styles and their listening patterns that will give you an idea about how they differ:

- People who are analytic and detailed-oriented want to hear a rational plan—the facts and the specifics. They listen for what's wrong.

- People who are action- and results-oriented listen for logic and speed. They want to hear what and when something is going to get done. They listen for the success factors.

- People who are highly social want to hear the personal connection. They listen for optimistic, positive ideas.

■ People who are steady, reliable team players want to hear the plan and how they will be supported in implementing it. They listen for appreciation and personal assurances.

If you listen deeply, you will be able to *hear* what people want and need, and then you will know how to respond effectively. Moreover, with better listening skills, you'll hear what your own intuition tells you and will know how to respond appropriately in any given situation.

Building Trust Requires Listening

If you want to build trust, listen to your people. When people feel that their leader doesn't hear or understand them, trust is diminished. In the previous chapter, we talked about the ability to build trust as a component of emotional intelligence. Listening on a deep level to others helps build trust. I've watched teams go through hellish periods together and remain bonded, because they knew they could count on their leader. Trust is the glue that keeps a team and an organization together. It doesn't matter how many team-building workshops a team has gone through, if team members don't have faith and trust that their leader is there to listen to their needs, and to find ways to support them, protect them, and help them achieve their goals, the team will become demotivated and performance will drop.

The Art of Asking Powerful Questions

Once you have mastered the art of listening, your next step is to master the art of inquiry—asking powerful questions. If you know how to ask powerful questions, it can help you solve problems, manage difficult conversations, and shape skillful conversation on an ongoing basis, empowering you and your team members.

Powerful questions are simple questions that arise out of a place of curiosity and carry with them the intent of learning. The strength of this type of inquiry comes from its ability to elicit more authentic, descriptive responses and to empower people to think in a way that leads them to action. The goal of a powerful question is to open up space for learning, new possibilities, and new solutions. Coaches ask powerful questions all the time. They are a staple in our tool boxes.

Powerful questions are open-ended "what" or "how" questions that are usually short (and seemingly even "dumb"): "What outcome do you want?" "What does that mean for you?" "How do you want to proceed?" These questions appear simple on the surface, but if they are asked at the right time, they can cause people to become more introspective and reflective. They impact people, deepening and expanding their thought processes, and cause people to think about an issue in a new way. A powerful question gets to the heart of the matter right away. It provides focus, clarity, and insight. "What" and "how" questions, as opposed to "why" questions, prevent people from becoming defensive. Powerful questions also support collaboration, because they enable everyone involved in the conversation to learn. They are great tools to use with teams in problem solving, because they arise from true curiosity. They make people stop and think. Powerful questions are nonjudgmental; there is no right or wrong answer. A simple "What would that get us?" frees up people to contemplate possibilities, leading to greater creativity.

A common misconception about leaders is that they have to know all the answers. No one person has the ability to know everything, especially in today's complex world. If you want to be an integrated leader, it's important for you to recognize that you don't need to know all the answers—just the right questions to ask. And you have to ask them in ways that will get people to think outside the box, respond more openly, and connect more with you and with each other.

Skillful Conversations: An Optimum Tool for Communicating

If you can ask powerful questions and then listen deeply to the responses, you will be one step closer to being an assertive communicator. When you talk with someone about a sensitive issue or an area of disagreement, or when members of your team are at odds, try having a skillful conversation. Conducted properly, it will open up space for understanding, for problem solving, and for learning how to move forward together.

Here's how to shape the conversation. First begin by focusing on the facts on which you both agree. What do you both know to be true? What data can't be misinterpreted? For example, let's say Tom and Barbara, peers on the same team, are working on a report that's due on the 15th of the month. It's now late afternoon on the 13th. Barbara likes to finish her work early and have time for last-minute changes—pushing close to a deadline causes her a great amount of stress. She is starting to get aggravated with Tom, because the report hasn't been completed and she believes that it's his fault.

Tom, on the other hand, is fairly laid back. He doesn't get stressed out easily, and he doesn't mind working under pressure. He's operating under the assumption that Barbara still has a piece of the report left to do, and he wants to wait until after he gets that piece from her to finish his part.

Rather than fussing and fuming in silence or acting out in some passive-aggressive way, Barbara needs to talk with Tom about the situation. A key principle in assertive communication is to address an issue immediately without letting it fester. Barbara needs to start a conversation, and she needs to start it from a point on which they both agree: from a fact that is observable by both of them. For instance, the report is due the 15th—the date is on their calendars. There are sections that are not yet complete—they can both see that. So, Barbara can say to Tom, "I need to have a conversation with you about our report. It's due on the 15th, and there are still sections that aren't complete."

The next step is to balance advocacy with inquiry. Inquiry, as we said earlier, is asking a powerful question in order to deepen understanding. When we inquire about another's perspective, we make the other person's reasoning visible. In this case, Barbara can ask Tom, "What do you see as the problem? How come we're at this point and we haven't finished yet?" Framing the question this way gives him an opportunity to explain his understanding and thinking, rather than pushing him into a defensive corner. When inquiring, use powerful questions such as, "What do you think of the situation?" "How does this make you feel?" "What possibilities do you see?"

Remember the way you frame a question sets the tone for the conversation. Questions open up space, which "judging" and "blaming" statements don't do. If Barbara had said, "You always do things at the last minute," or "You never seem to care if things get done on time," she would be pushing Tom into a defensive stance. Frame your conversations to focus on specific behaviors, rather than on vague personality traits. When people feel personally attacked, they will either completely retreat or come out fighting, reducing the likelihood that they will really hear each other and find a good solution.

After listening attentively to the other person's responses, advocate for your position. Advocacy is communicating in a way that makes your reasoning visible to the other person. In this part of the conversation, you describe your position so that the other person can understand your perspective. Stay grounded and confident, demonstrating your power by the manner in which you speak and the words you choose. When you are advocating, use "I" language and state your position in a clear, precise way. For example, Barbara could say, "We're close to deadline and the report's not done. I feel like we're in a jam, which makes me worried and angry. I have been waiting for you and I don't understand what the hold up is."

Provide the rationale for why you feel the way you do. This is the place where you get to talk about your beliefs, feelings, and emotions. It's okay to have feelings and talk about them as long as you talk about them in *non-emotional, rational* ways.

Sometimes you will want to advocate for yourself before you make inquiries about the other person, but it really depends on the situation. Just go back and forth, balancing advocacy and inquiry so that the full story emerges and you can both surface any erroneous assumptions and beliefs. This process of dialogue enables collaboration to take place and encourages the people involved to participate in problem solving. Problems arise when there is miscommunication resulting from misperceptions about what's really going on, what's really happening, and what people are really thinking and feeling. Barbara thought Tom was responsible for the section, and Tom was waiting for Barbara.

Make sure you have identified what outcomes you want and what outcomes the other person wants. Continue asking questions to explore the other person's beliefs, perceptions, feelings, and needs, and paraphrase from time to time until you feel that you have the full story laid out. Look for a mutually satisfying solution by talking about a variety of options, acknowledging the problems and the benefits. When you come to an agreement, repeat back your understanding of the agreement for clarity. How many times have you ended a conversation thinking you were on the same page, only to discover later on that you both heard the agreement in different ways? Close the conversation with a commitment to some kind of action.

You might need to make a clear direct request of the other person in order to ensure that the agreement will be acted on. For example, once Tom and Barbara cleared up their misconceptions, they agreed that the report could get finished on time and that Tom didn't need more information from Barbara to finish his section. However, Barbara wanted to see the final document before Tom submitted it, so she made the request that he give it to her by noon the following day—in time for her to review it and make any last-minute changes. By making a precise request and getting Tom to commit to it, Barbara prevented further misinterpretations and made it more likely that they would turn the report in on time (with less stress for Barbara).

A request, however, can be rejected or countered. Tom might have said, "I can't guarantee I'll get it to you by noon, but I'll make sure you have it by 2:00 P.M." By using the framework for a skillful conversation, Barbara and Tom were able to move ahead together to achieve results with deeper understanding and mutual respect for each other's needs.

I coach my clients to hold skillful conversations and to use this tool with their teams. It's particularly helpful for situations when direct reports are in conflict with each other. Post the steps on a flipchart and use them as a guideline to facilitate a skillful conversation between people who are having difficulties working together.

A Framework for a Skillful Conversation
Start with data. Describe what's happening.
Inquire about the other person's position. Ask *powerful* questions.
Advocate your position using "I" language.
Acknowledge for connection.
Paraphrase and summarize for clarity.
Look for a mutually satisfying solution.
Make a clear request, and get commitment.

Negotiation: Taking Skillful Conversations to the Next Level

Leaders are called upon every day to negotiate something: budgets, goals, resources, or some other issue. So, negotiation is not just about making some high-level deal or providing a solution to a hotly disputed issue. People in flattened organizations need to influence one another and come to some kind of negotiated agreement on just about everything. In this respect, negotiation is similar to holding a skillful conversation—it's about managing relationships and moving forward to resolve a situation in a mutually successful way.

In a negotiation, it's important to gather as much information as possible ahead of time. The more prepared you are and the more knowledge you have about the other person's wants, needs, and bottom line, the greater chance you will have to frame your negotiation in a way that will make it successful.

In *Shadow Negotiations*, authors Deborah Kolb and Judith Williams point out that in every negotiation, there is a parallel negotiation taking place that goes beyond the issue being discussed. This "shadow" negotiation has to do with the relationship between the two parties. If the real issues are not clearly on the table, people will be distracted from them and will focus on the un-named shadow or relationship issues.

According to Kolb, in order to create conditions for a successful negotiation, you must do the following:

Know what you want

Understand your strengths and vulnerabilities

Learn as much as you can about the other person's wants, needs, and bottom line

Create the space to build rapport and connect with the other person

Frame the agenda by being both firm and flexible

Have a variety of options to offer

Turn challenges that put you on the defensive or at a disadvantage by naming, questioning, correcting, or diverting them

This last step will depend on how assertively you're communicating. In order to turn challenges around, you need to think on your feet and be assertive enough to ask the right questions, divert attacks, name the moves you see the other person taking, and point out errors and correct them.

Advocating for Yourself

In a negotiation, it's essential that you advocate for yourself. In leadership, it's also essential. I've had clients who have struggled with this concept, feeling that advocating for themselves is self-aggrandizing, egotistical, and offensive. But to grow as a leader, it's important to believe in your abilities and be able to talk confidently about your skills and strengths. This doesn't mean that you should lose your humility, but remember that if you cannot advocate for yourself and your ideas, you will not garner the visibility you need for assignments that will help you advance as a leader.

To grow your leadership, it's critical for you to make yourself visible—to have your work recognized and acknowledged. So pay attention to your strengths: continually enhance and leverage them, and communicate your value to the right people.

I've worked with numbers of clients who had trouble advocating for themselves and getting their bosses to recognize their contributions. One client, whom I'll call Vicky, came to me because she was having a problem getting her boss to understand the full range of value she had been adding to the organization. She and her boss were not located in the same geographic area, and he didn't see her on a day-to-day or even a week-to-week basis. This can be a problem if managers and team members are located around the globe or don't otherwise work in a face-to-face environment.

Vicky's boss wasn't conducting timely performance evaluations, so he didn't know how much work she did, how varied it was, how much time it took, or how successful she was at managing all of it. Through coaching, Vicky realized that in order to give him the full scope of her efforts and results, she needed to create a weekly written report that could be e-mailed to him. She also needed to request regular one-on-one sessions—weekly or bi-weekly, or at least monthly. Just taking those two small steps helped her enormously in getting her work recognized. Vicky wasn't trying to brag about herself; she was simply opening up communication channels that benefited her, but also helped her boss.

Other ways to gain visibility might call for you to stretch and take risks. You can ask to lead a cross-functional team, for example, or join a high profile task force, take on an important project, run an off-site meeting, or develop a new program. All of these activities require you to be an assertive communicator who can talk about your skills and advocate for yourself.

Managing Evaluations

If you are not receiving performance evaluations on a regular basis, create monthly, quarterly, bi-weekly, or weekly reports that track your activities and accomplish-ments, and submit them to your boss. These reports provide a way for you to track your own activities and see for yourself how good you are. They give you a communication vehicle for making your results and your successes visible, and they can help your boss when it comes time to do a review. Your boss won't have to scramble to remember what you've done—the reports will provide a recording of the activities and outcomes you want acknowledged. Written properly, your reports can even provide the language you want your boss to use when evaluating you. Having a written record of your accomplishments can also be extremely valuable if you ever have to defend yourself against unfair accusations.

Then do the same thing with your direct reports: Have them present you with regular reports and biannual or annual self-evaluations and hold frequent one-on-one meetings throughout the year to discuss their performance.

Being assertive also means being able to agree to disagree in a respectful manner. If you are given a performance evaluation that you don't agree with, don't sign off on it out of frustration or because you just want it over and done with. Once you have signed off on something, you have agreed on paper to what is being said about you, and you lose your power to refute criticisms at a later date. I'm not saying that you shouldn't accept valid constructive criticism—that's what performance evaluations are for: to help you see yourself as others see you so that you can improve your skills. You gain power and improve as a leader when you demonstrate your commitment to continued performance improvement by acknowledging which competencies you need to work on and develop. However, if there is something in the evaluation that you think is misguided or downright wrong and you *don't* refute it, you will limit your ability in the future to explain a difference in perspective. If you can't get the evaluation modified or changed, take the time to write out a thorough response on the evaluation before you sign it. Stick to the facts. Don't ramble. Don't be emotional, and don't attack or criticize anyone else. Just make it clear that you disagree with the evaluation, and succinctly present your perspective. Ask to have your response included in your file.

If you are doing a self-evaluation, don't be modest. You know what you are really good at—write it down. Ask yourself two questions: *"What do I want to accomplish with this performance evaluation?"* and *"What do I need to say about myself—about my skills, strengths, and talents—that will help me accomplish my evaluation goal?"* Again, stay focused on yourself. This is about *you*.

When it comes to evaluating your own developmental needs, try not to describe your weaknesses in detail. Instead, describe the kind of support you believe would be helpful to you in enhancing your performance. For example, mention some courses you would like to take or some projects you would like to be involved in that will help you to improve a skill that needs strengthening.

Sometimes people are brutally honest about their own developmental needs. I've worked with women who have remembered every flaw and every mistake they had ever made, and believed that they should expose all their imperfections. Know how to maintain your boundaries and how much information to share. The goal is to obtain support for your own development as a leader, not to shoot yourself in the foot!

Gender Differences in Communicating

I often hear people (mostly women) talk about how they hold back when it comes to letting others know that they are competent, skilled, and talented. Many believe that all they have to do is perform well and they will be rewarded. But you have to let *the right people* know how good you are. If you don't advocate for yourself, who's going to? If you don't speak up for yourself, why would you expect someone else to speak up for you?

Communication is one area in which gender differences definitely emerge. Deborah Tannen, author of several best sellers, writes extensively on this topic. According to Tannen, when we communicate across genders, we are communicating cross-culturally and are trying to balance the conflicting needs of involvement and independence. Women tend to look for equality and communicate to involve others, while men seek to demonstrate independence and communicate to establish themselves. Women can find it more difficult to advocate for themselves because it sets them apart from others, while men tell you what they want you to know to demonstrate their uniqueness. If you are a woman, the obvious catch is that if you can't tell men what's unique about you, they are likely to think there isn't anything.

I've also noticed that men don't seem to get into the minutiae of negative self-analysis the way women do, analyzing and re-analyzing every aspect and nuance of a conversation or situation (especially if they made a mistake). Women will agonize over what was said and what they did wrong. Paradoxically, while women have trouble advocating for themselves, they have no trouble confessing all their mistakes to anyone who will listen.

There are many more gender-communication differences. Some differences are obvious: Men tend to speak more at meetings and interrupt more; women tend to make more direct eye contact and ask more questions. Other differences are less obvious, but carry with them implications about power and confidence. Even when men and women speak the same way, they can be judged differently. So, what does this mean? It means it's critical that men and women educate themselves about gender differences in communication so that they can present themselves better, understand each other better, and stop making incorrect assumptions and interpretations.

I'm not in favor of women trying to be like men or men trying to be like women, but we can learn from each other. One type of learning leads to another: The more aware you are about how gender affects you and the way you behave and communicate, the better prepared you will be to integrate masculine and feminine energy. By plugging in to both the feminine and masculine, you can learn how to be more well rounded without sacrificing who you are. The more fully integrated you are, the more likely you will reach your full potential and become the powerful leader you were meant to be.

Leadership Requires Setting Expectations and Giving Feedback

Two other communication skills critical for good leadership are setting expectations and providing feedback for others. As a leader, it's your responsibility to be clear about people's roles and goals and what you expect from each individual. It's up to you not only to articulate your strategic vision, but also to communicate clearly how you expect people to fulfill it. If you are fuzzy about what you want from people, they will flounder. They need to hear from you, and you need to make sure they understand you.

If you haven't set clear expectations, you won't be able to provide accurate feedback. The goal of giving feedback is to help another individual grow and develop. Your comments are meant to help the other person, but if you can't clearly communicate what you expect or how well those expectations were met, you won't be able to help people improve or achieve specific goals.

Many people complain about bosses who micro-manage, but it is just as disconcerting to have a boss who is so hands-off that you never know what she's thinking or how well you're doing. When managers don't offer feedback on a regular basis to their team or to direct reports, it can affect morale and plant seeds of uncertainty and insecurity. Most of us want guidance and recognition. Even high performers can start to feel confused if they are not told that they are doing a good job or are on the right track. Lack of acknowledgment and recognition can eventually create resentment, which leads to loss of motivation.

Leaders who are too hands-off can create even greater problems when they don't stay on top of people who are on learning and growth curves. Small problems or difficulties can rapidly escalate into crisis situations and spread like wildfire. A leader with too much of a hands-off style can find herself up to her elbows in problems that take a lot of energy to solve and that leave a path of destruction, requiring lots of time to repair.

The key is to empower team members to do their work, but to keep two-way lines of communication open and flowing. As a leader, you should be aware of what all your team members are doing and whether or not their projects are aligned with your strategic goals. I had a client who thought he was empowering his team by standing back and letting them make decisions for themselves. However, he didn't make his expectations explicit about the kinds of decisions team members could make for themselves and which ones they needed to clear with him. It was only after they had rolled out a major project on their own that he discovered how "hands-off" he had become. The project had all kinds of holes in it—flaws that reflected poorly on him and the team—and it took a great deal of time to get everything straightened out.

To make sure your team is on track, make sure you are giving team members the guidance they need and provide them with performance feedback on a regular basis. Let them know what you expect and what your goals are. Then, in an open, honest, and direct way, let them know what you feel is working and what's not. Point out their strengths, and when they're successful, congratulate them. Offer special rewards for really good performance—it's amazing what pizza and beer can do for people.

When things aren't going well, ask people what they think is the cause of the problem. Be respectful of them and listen to their answers. Be explicit and specific, and provide examples of behavior that call for improvement. Then provide guidance on steps they can take to change those behaviors. Always address the issues and behaviors, rather than criticize the person. For example, if someone's work is messy and prone to error, instead of accusing her of being careless and lazy, point out the frequency of her errors and ask her what behavior she needs to change in order to make fewer mistakes. What's happening that she's making so many errors? Does she understand the work? Does she have enough knowledge? What does she need to do to be more accurate and catch mistakes?

It's your job as a leader to stay involved and provide regular feedback. Meet with your team on a regular basis and create an environment of trust and honesty where people can come to you for advice and guidance on small things before they grow into big problems.

Managing "No"

Being assertive also means that you don't get negatively influenced by the word "no." Assertive communicators don't get frightened when people say "no," nor are they afraid of saying "no" to others.

There's a great story that I tell over and over in my workshops about a Texas Instruments vice president who didn't take "no" for an answer. Earlier in her career with the company, her business unit started to decline sharply. She saw the writing on the wall and began asking senior management to move her out of the unit and into a division that would not only benefit from her talents and skills, but that would also keep her career alive within the company. Senior managers in her division, however, were more focused on what was happening to the unit than on the individuals in it, and her requests to be transferred were continually turned down. She finally realized that she had to develop a different strategy. Rather than hounding the managers within her business unit, she began introducing herself to senior managers in other divisions of the corporation. She began cold-calling senior executives across the organization to set up informational meetings. During each brief meeting, she described her skills and strengths and made a simple request of the executive: "If there is an opening in your department that requires someone with my talents and skills, please consider me for the position." She says it was the bravest career move she had ever made.

Her strategy paid off, and within a short amount of time, she received a phone call to interview in another division. She landed the job, and eventually climbed to the level of vice president within that division. She was able to hear "no" in a way that she didn't interpret as an assault on her competencies, and her understanding of the business environment and culture enabled her to shape and communicate a clear message about her skills and goals. These two things gave her a great deal of power in terms of developing her leadership and moving herself forward.

The lesson here is that "no" is just a word. It's how you interpret its meaning that can screw you up. "No" can be a very empowering word: By virtue of making a request, you have moved yourself into a new space. If your request is denied, all you have to do is think up a different strategy and make another request. Leadership is about having the drive to succeed.

The word "no" is also powerful, and you need to know how to use it yourself. Integrated leaders set good boundaries and are clear about what they'll do or not do. Learning how to handle a "no" means being able to hear it without taking it personally, but also to say it without being concerned that you are offending the other person. A leader knows how to say "no" and respects others by recognizing that they, too, have the maturity to handle it.

Assertiveness Summary Steps

Poor listening skills, confusing communication, and mixed messages are at the heart of many of our problems. If you truly want to be an integrated leader, you must develop your ability to communicate assertively. Practice listening carefully and attentively to enhance your understanding and to build trust. Harness your curiosity and ask powerful questions when you're trying to solve problems or uncover the heart of an issue. Hold skillful conversations in order to generate learning, deepen understanding, and reach mutually agreeable resolutions. Set clear expectations, and give constructive feedback to help your team develop and grow. Maintain your boundaries and treat yourself and others with respect. Stay grounded by maintaining control over your emotions, remain confident, and over time your assertive communication skills will help you develop the presence of a leader.

Coaching Questions on Assertive Communication

Answer the following questions, reflecting on what you need to do to be a more assertive communicator.

What are your listening barriers?

What do you listen for? What can you do to listen on a deeper level?

How effective are you at asking powerful questions? What do you need to do to be more effective?

How good are you at holding a skillful conversation? What do you need to practice to become more skillful?

How assertive are you as a communicator? What do you need to do to be more assertive?

What does "no" mean to you? How does your interpretation help or hinder you in communicating?

How good are you at advocating for yourself? What can you do to improve?

(continued)

Coaching Questions on
Assertive Communication *(concluded)*

How effective are you at influencing others? What can you do to improve?

How effective are you at negotiating? What do you need to do to become better?

What kind of visibility do you have? Who needs to know about your performance? How can you communicate with them and make yourself visible?

How effective are you at setting expectations and providing feedback? What do you need to do to be more effective?

How effective are you at communicating across genders? What do you need to do to get a better understanding of gender and cultural differences?

What type of message does your body language send? How can you improve your body language?

What kind of "presence" do you have? What can you do to enhance it?

CHAPTER FIVE
Be Connected:
Build Strategic Relationships

You can succeed on your own terms, but you can't succeed alone—you need other people. Building strategic relationships is the fifth key strategy for coaching yourself to leadership. It's helpful to first develop the other four strategies—to identify your values, to create your vision, to build your emotional intelligence, and to hone your assertive communication skills—because they will help you make connections and develop relationships that will support your growth as a leader.

To build strategic relationships, you must first know which people you should be developing relationships with, and then find ways to connect and build alliances with those people. To be a successful leader, it will be essential for you to establish and maintain trusting relationships with significant people above, below, and around you. In addition, you'll need strong relationships with customers, vendors, suppliers, and mentors. It takes a strategic network of diverse contacts to advance your career and develop yourself as a leader.

Alliance Building: Is There Something to Learn from Reality Shows?

I admit I'm a junky when it comes to two reality shows: "Survivor" and "The Apprentice." Although they are heavily edited, they demonstrate the power of alliances and give us a captivating peek at the dynamics of human interaction—the good, the bad, the beautiful, and the ugly. On these shows, we see what happens when people try to work together in a competitive environment. As groups move through the competition, there is something new to learn as each team creates its own unique group dynamic based on the different players.

In both shows, we see what happens when people are separated into tribes or teams. We witness the intensity of the pull and tug created when tribes and teams merge, and we can see the struggle that each person goes through when his or her fragile sense of belonging is uprooted. Similar struggles happen daily in the business world as companies merge, acquire, or restructure, and teams have to come together to meet organizational goals.

According to psychologist Abraham Maslow, only when lower-level needs of physiological well-being, safety, and a sense of belonging are met can we successfully meet higher-level, self-esteem needs of competence, achievement, status, and fulfillment. It's critically important as human beings to have this sense of belonging and affiliation with others. It anchors us and gives us the ability to develop and grow. The people we are aligned with at any given time can either help us in our development or cause us a huge amount of consternation.

As I watch both these shows and observe people at work, the lesson gets drummed home that it isn't always what you know, but *who* you know and how well you work together that can determine your fate. In "The Apprentice," the final winners definitely demonstrate skill and ability, but along the way we see that it also matters whether or not they were good team players. In the boardroom, contestants need other team members to support and defend them to Donald

Trump. In "Survivor," skill plays a role and can win immunity for players, protecting them from being voted off the island (and, thus, giving them a better shot at the money), but immunity alone doesn't do the trick. Luck and timing play a part. But ultimately, in the end, it's the other players who determine the winner.

In "Survivor," the integrity and character of the final contestants usually come into play—people are judged for lying and breaking trusted agreements. Some players justify whatever they do because they believe that it's just a game and it's necessary to do whatever it takes to win. Some people have the same feeling about business. But in these shows and in the business world, the relationships a player has forged, and the extent to which he or she honors those alliances sways the final outcome.

Many people shy away from the need to build alliances, and aren't even sure it fits into their value system. Women in particular tend to believe that if they just do their jobs well, they will be rewarded. They equate orchestrating relationships with manipulation and believe it will compromise their integrity. They don't want to play office politics.

In developing your leadership potential, however, remember that you have to orchestrate your own game. You do need to figure out with whom you should align, and which individuals will provide you with the right kind of support. You need to know whom you can trust and whose strengths complement yours. If you know your values and what you want, if you are emotionally intelligent and know how to communicate assertively, the alliances you build will be beneficial to you and to others. You will be able to maintain your authenticity and your integrity by taking responsibility for your actions and treating others as you want to be treated.

When building relationships, use your emotional intelligence and control your emotions. Group and organizational politics can get nasty if people allow their emotions to rule their behavior. Think before you speak—be discerning about what you say and don't say. Your words can heighten your status, or haunt you forever. Don't lie, but that doesn't mean you have to tell *everything* to *everyone*. And don't play people against each other—you can play fair and still play smart. You can play an honest game and win, but you can't win alone.

Lessons in Alliance Building

Now that you understand what alliance building has to do with leadership, start developing alliances by first thinking in win/win terms. Take time to plan and think strategically when developing your network of relationships. You are not being scheming or callous. You are simply assessing your situation and building the kind of mutually beneficial relationships that will help you achieve your goals. Use the exercise on the following page to help identify the people with whom you should build relationships. Remember that relationship building should be reciprocal: both you and the other person should benefit, even in some small way, from the collaboration. Sometimes it is not immediately evident what someone else can gain from being in a relationship with you, particularly if the other person is more powerful or better connected than you are, but every emotionally healthy relationship offers us the opportunity to learn and grow.

When you think about building new relationships, be selective. You want to align yourself with trustworthy people, so screen each person and be discerning. Look for people inside and outside your company, people in your function and outside it, people who are strategists, and people who can show you how to implement your strategy to reach your goals. Basically, you want a network of people who together can help you get where you want to go.

Although I said you won't succeed on skills and knowledge alone, don't misunderstand: intelligence is a critical component of leadership, and performance definitely counts. You need to perform well and have people recognize your worth. No one wants to be affiliated with a loser. We all want to have relationships with people who add value to our own experience, and who can help us move forward.

Building Alliances Exercise

As you think about developing your leadership, think about the relationships that would be helpful to you and ask yourself the following questions:

Whom can I learn from?

Whom do I admire, respect, and wish to emulate?

Who can help me advance my career?

Who can connect me with other significant people?

Who can help me expand my area of influence?

Who has access to significant resources and information?

Who can learn from me?

Whom can I help?

What do I have to offer?

What value do I bring?

Mentors: A Critical Alliance

One of the most critical alliances you can form is with a senior manager who is willing to mentor you. Research indicates mentoring is a truly powerful way to develop leadership ability. When it comes to women's leadership, a lack of mentors has been one of the barriers that has held women back in the past. Mentors are role models who offer the wisdom of their experience. A mentor provides valuable feedback that can help you navigate turbulent political organizational waters, gain entry to key people, and smooth out your career climb.

While researching my 1998 book, *Success on Our Own Terms*, I discovered that 44 out of the 45 women managers and executives from Fortune 500 companies who I interviewed had mentors who were critical to their success. These mentors helped them navigate their organizations by opening doors for them and making introductions, assisting them in selecting and obtaining the right positions, and guiding them with advice and counsel. The woman who had the greatest difficulty moving her career forward lacked a mentor. It took her seven years to transition out of her position as a programmer into marketing. During much of that time, she felt more frustrated than empowered. Had she had the support of a mentor from the beginning of her career, her path up and out of programming would most likely have been much quicker and easier.

I didn't have a mentor earlier in my career, and I made a number of questionable career choices. I didn't know where to go for help, and I didn't even know the questions I should have been asking. Without a mentor and someone to give me feedback and encouragement, I allowed my insecurities to get the better of me. We need other people to support us in our journey. Sometimes, we literally can't see the forest for the trees—we get blinded by our own issues and perceptions. We need others to help us see *all* the possibilities more clearly. This is one of the key reasons why I became a coach—to support others and give them the kind of help that I wish I had had when I started building my career.

Mentors Make Things Happen

Your boss can mentor you, but it's better to have mentors who are one or two layers above your boss. Then if things go wrong in your relationship with your boss, you'll have someone more powerful to support you.

One of my clients, whom I'll call Monica, was having a great deal of trouble with her boss. The two of them just kept butting heads. When Monica came to me, she had pretty much decided that she was just going to give up, and sit back and wait for retirement. However, retirement was still six years off (which is a long time to do nothing). Moreover, Monica's personality simply didn't match with that image. If anything, she is the type of person who likes to be involved; she also tends to press on issues and wants to be heard.

We worked on a number of strategies, and Monica soon learned how to communicate in a more powerful, assertive way. Several months after we had finished our coaching sessions, she called me up to share some exciting news. She had met one of the most senior leaders in her corporation while working on a task force, and after two or three meetings with him, she asked him if he would mentor her. He immediately agreed, and began challenging her to set and attain higher goals. Bolstered by his support, Monica approached her job with new vigor and faith in herself. She also gained an unexpected bonus from her relationship with him: Her boss's attitude toward her started changing. The fact that one of the top execs thought enough of Monica to mentor her began to influence her boss's perception of her.

People started to see her in a different light, and her new empowered sense of herself helped to reinforce their new perceptions.

How I Met My Mentor

When I started my coaching practice, I immediately began looking for mentors who were also professional coaches. I met Sydney Rice Harrild, whom I mentioned in Chapter One, shortly after *Success on Our Own Terms* was published. I was presenting at a women's business conference at which women business owners were given space to display their products and promotional material. Sydney ended up with an undesirable spot in the back of the room that received little traffic. Undaunted, she picked up her brochures and moved to a highly visible spot in the hallway. As women passed her, she greeted them warmly and handed them her well-designed brochure. I was struck by her demeanor and her material, and thought she might be a good person for me to know.

About a week after the conference, I called her up, introduced myself, and asked if I could take her to lunch. She had heard me present and was impressed by the research I had done for my book. She wanted to learn more about my experience because she was just beginning to write her own book, *Choice Points*. Sydney became one of my key mentors, connecting me with numerous people who have since helped me to advance my business. Over the years, our relationship has flourished and changed as we take turns mentoring each other.

Finding and Nurturing
Mentoring Relationships

Finding a mentor isn't necessarily an easy thing to do. Many people get stymied by the process. Start by doing your homework. Look for people you admire who are several levels above you in your organization and people you respect in your external environment, such as leaders in your trade or professional associations.

Make sure potential mentors are competent and experienced and recognized for their leadership, knowledge, experience, and wisdom. Basically, you want someone who is highly successful. You also want mentors who have values similar to yours—people whom you respect and trust—so that you will feel comfortable confiding in them and taking advice from them. They should be approachable and transmit a feeling that they are willing to advocate for you and to share their experiences with you.

Since a mentor's role is to act as your guide, assisting you in setting goals and planning strategies to help you develop your career and your leadership skills, you want someone who is emotionally intelligent—someone who knows how to manage his or her own emotions and knows how to help you manage yours. Great communication and coaching skills are also essential. Your mentor needs to be a good listener who can hear what you are saying and can give you feedback that you can hear and understand. Your mentor should also know how to help you reframe issues so that you can see new possibilities and solutions.

When you first contact potential mentors, here's a good way to open the conversation: First, tell them what you admire about them and their work. Ask if they have time to answer some of your questions and to share some of their experiences with you. Then share something unique about yourself. Have your introduction honed to perfection so that you can quickly talk about your talents and skills in a way that catches their attention and makes them want to know more about you. During your conversation, pay attention to the feelings and energy you're picking up to determine if the fit feels right. But wait until you've gotten to know people before you ask them to mentor you—give yourself some time to see how the chemistry between you develops.

It's good to have more than one mentor. Ideally, you should have several at any given time, with each person offering a different kind of support. One person can't know everything, so look at the kinds of expertise and support you need, and build relationships with a variety of successful people. It's also a good idea to have both male and female mentors so that you get a well-rounded perspective. This is especially true for women who might still be surrounded by men in their jobs. Women in these circumstances find it particularly helpful to have women mentors to role model what it means to be a female leader.

It's also best to have informal as well as formal mentors. There is a difference between the two: A formal mentoring relationship has guidelines, goals, and boundaries, while an informal relationship is more casual. When you have found someone you want to enter into a formal mentoring relationship with, set up guidelines for the relationship so that both of you are clear on responsibilities and expectations. You should identify clear goals for developing your career and leadership, but also goals for the relationship: How do you both want to benefit? Successful mentoring relationships are learning experiences for the person being mentored *and* the mentor. I am always learning from the people I coach.

To ensure that boundaries of the relationship are respected, create a mutually agreeable structure that spells out the frequency of contact and method of communication.

How often will you talk? Will you talk on the phone, or meet in person? What about some combination of the two? How about e-mail? While I don't advocate coaching or mentoring exclusively online, e-mail as a communication tool shouldn't be overlooked, because it is easy and fast. However, get clear about how often it's acceptable to send e-mails to your mentor and what kind of response is expected. And finally, determine how long the relationship will last. It's also important to agree on how you will end the relationship if it starts to go sour. Since both parties are expected to benefit from the relationship, both of you need to feel free to say that it's not working. Having a structure in place makes it easier to come to a resolution.

Managing Up: Building a Good Relationship with Your Boss

The relationship you have with your boss is critical. The quality of your relationship definitely affects your well-being as well as your ability to develop your leadership skills and your career.

The first step in building a good relationship with your boss is to know what's important to her. What are her strategic goals? You should be very clear about her goals and objectives so that you can ensure that your work is aligned around those goals. It's your responsibility to support your boss by delivering what she needs you to deliver. It's your job to perform well and bring in the necessary results.

The next step is to be clear about your boss's expectations. What does she want from you? What are *your* goals and objectives? How will she measure your performance?

Another helpful step is to understand her behavioral and communication styles. How does she like to receive information? What does she listen for when she's communicating with you? What makes her happy? What gets her angry? What do you do that ticks her off? What is her perception of you?

Use your emotional intelligence to see situations from your boss's perspective and to focus on her good qualities. If you have a difficult boss and you focus on the negative, you'll get caught up in the negative energy and end up engaging in a tug of war (which you are far more likely to lose than she is). So, identify and acknowledge your boss's good characteristics and give her some stroking, no matter how difficult that is.

Dealing with a Difficult Boss

At one time or another, most of us have dealt with a difficult boss. When there are difficulties in the relationship, make sure that your behaviors are not making the situation worse. What part do you play in it? What are you being stubborn about? What can you do differently? What can you let go of? What accommodations can you make? Figure out what the ideal resolution would be and what steps you can take toward that resolution.

Be clear about what's happening between the two of you, and set boundaries around what you will or won't tolerate. If you have a demanding boss and start feeling frustrated and insecure, your boss will pick up on this and might use it to his advantage. Don't allow yourself to be taken advantage of. Once an aggressive boss realizes that he can push you around, he'll push you even more, and lose respect for you. You'll then find yourself in a downward spiral becoming more and more insecure and getting taken advantage of more and more.

Do *not* accept abusive behavior. When you feel your boss is being abusive, initiate a conversation and point out the specific behaviors that are unacceptable. If you have a boss who screams and yells, you can simply tell him that you won't continue the conversation until he stops yelling. Chronicle the abuse, and keep records. Make sure you inform HR of abusive behavior in a timely manner.

If you have a passive-aggressive boss who is skilled at tripping you up in subtle ways, be very careful. This is a person you really should not trust. Be wary of what he says, because as I pointed out in the previous chapter, the passive-aggressive person sends mixed messages that can be loaded with hidden agendas. Make sure you document your results and achievements and any agreements you make. Double-check with him as you move forward with projects to make sure he's still singing the same tune he sang the last time you came to an agreement. Make sure you are providing him with what he wants. Be as clear as possible. Get agreements in writing: Send him written project outlines and progress reports, and request timely feedback. Again, set firm boundaries. Don't allow yourself to get hooked. Keep an emotional distance, and learn from the experience.

If you've tried everything and nothing seems to work, figure out how long you can tolerate the situation without stressing yourself to a breaking point. You shouldn't let one person push you from a company, but if there is nowhere else within the organization to move, you might need to consider leaving. It's one thing to tolerate the heat and learn how to work with difficult people, but don't allow yourself to get burned.

Building Your Team:
The Ultimate Test of Leadership

Leaders are certainly judged on the quality of their teams, and their ability to lead them to success and achievement of their goals. Here's a simple but profound formula for becoming a good leader that a woman vice president at Hewlett-Packard gave me:

- **Create and hold the vision.** Let your people know where they are going. It's important for them to see the vision as clearly as you do.

- **Communicate the mission.** Explain why they are going there. Give them the rationale so that they understand the mission and why they need to do what they need to do.

- **Explain the strategy.** Provide them with guidance on how they are going to get there, and give them the resources they need to implement the strategy.

- **Demonstrate by your actions and your words that your people come before you.**

These steps sound fairly simple, but putting them into practice requires skill, passion, and a deep commitment to your team. As I said in an earlier chapter, good leadership skills are similar to good parenting skills. If you are a parent or a leader, you need to provide firm direction and guidance, and give your children and your team members the space to grow and make mistakes. You need to provide a sense of safety, even as you challenge them to move forward and "try on" new behaviors.

Since you are a role model, your energy and actions send messages that affect the people who report to you, and your passion inspires them. It's your energy and excitement that will motivate your team to attain the vision and accomplish the mission. You need to set clear, achievable goals and then provide the support and resources required to attain them. If you don't know where you're going or how you're going to get there, how will they? If your people don't have adequate resources to carry out their jobs, then you must help them prioritize so that they can do as much as possible given their constrictions. By providing them with support, you not only demonstrate that you care about getting the job done, but you also show that you care about *them*. People develop loyalty when they believe their needs are being considered. If your workers are overworked and overstressed, they are less likely to be committed to you. It's your responsibility to create a supportive environment.

Motivating Your Team

Your team members will become more committed, empowered, and motivated if they trust and feel that you make sacrifices yourself and put aside your own ego to act in their best interests. They'll have faith in you if you listen to and respect them, empathize with their perspectives, consider what they say, and continually share information in an open, honest manner. If you truly listen to them, you'll not only be able to pick up valuable information, but you'll also become aware of any negative vibrations long before things get out of hand.

Communication is so important that I devoted the previous chapter to it, but just to underscore the message once more, it's incumbent on you as a leader to be proactive and not reactive, and to address issues clearly, directly, and immediately so that problems don't fester and grow. Moreover, if team members have trust in you, they'll feel comfortable coming to you and being truthful about their concerns and doubts.

Likewise, your people will accept your directives and make sacrifices to attain goals if they trust and believe that you are telling them the truth. They'd rather hear the harsh reality than be placated with lies. If you are consistent and fair, as well as open and honest, people will know what to expect and how to behave. But if you demonstrate erratic behavior, and you don't "walk your talk," you can bet that the performance of your people will also be inconsistent. It's your responsibility to control your own behavior and not act emotionally and impulsively. Good morale and productivity tend to increase in a calm, fair environment. Just like children need to believe in and trust their parents, the people who work for you need to believe in and trust you. You won't be able to count on them unless they can count on you. They need to know that you will not compromise your own integrity, nor ask them to compromise theirs.

As an integrated leader, you should also know what kinds of rewards motivate your team. Monetary compensation is not the only motivator: flexibility and control over the way they do their work are huge motivators for many people, especially for women. People want to be able to adjust their schedules when necessary without having to make a big deal about it. They want their managers to trust that even if they need to come in late, leave early, or take time out during the day, they will get the job done. People also want acknowledgment for their efforts. My research tells me that respect and recognition far outrank money as a motivator for women. If you acknowledge people's efforts and support their success, they will try even harder to please you.

Integrated leaders know how to motivate their troops without resorting to fear and intimidation. People operating under a fear mentality are not able to give their all to their jobs, because part of their energy is being used to protect themselves. People respond much better to positive reinforcement than they do to negative criticism. The worry and stress that intimidation triggers gets in the way of efficiency and productivity. People are also more committed and willing to go the extra mile for a leader they respect and admire. Integrated leaders know what motivates their teams and they know how to leverage people's strengths.

The Story of Cheryl: A Partnership Approach to Team Building

The experience of one of my colleagues demonstrates the significance of building strong relationships. Cheryl is an organizational development and training director at a major university. She doubled revenue within her first two years by using what she refers to as a "partnership" approach to leadership. When Cheryl took this position, the environment within the organization was charged: the previous director had left abruptly and staff members weren't exactly sure why. She had estranged many employees, consultants, and customers with her autocratic style, but the team believed that senior management had unfairly pushed her out. When Cheryl came on board, team members were outwardly cooperative, but inwardly very angry and worried about their own positions. Morale was suffering greatly.

Cheryl has a relational and empowering style of leadership. She used her emotional intelligence and immediately focused on increasing communication, building relationships, and forging team decision making, but she was met with great skepticism, fear, and even hostility.

The first thing that Cheryl did was to focus on her staff and build a trusting relationship with them. She worked collaboratively with the team to develop the organization's vision, mission, and business plan and to begin building relationships with other stakeholders. Team members were given the space to develop themselves, define their own work environment, and create projects that really excited them. Cheryl wanted team members to enjoy creating new services that would enable them to improve their own leadership skills while meeting the needs of clients. Empowering them in this way increased their loyalty and productivity.

Motivation Exercise

Answer the following questions to see how well you know *your* team.

How often do you meet with your team as a whole? How often do you meet with team members individually?

What are the strengths and developmental areas of each member of your team?

What is each member doing for his or her own development?

What is each member of your team presently working on with regard to the team's goals? What is the status of progress?

What resources does the team need to fulfill its goals?

What do you need to do to help them excel?

What motivates your team as a whole?

What motivates team members on an individual level?

What do you need to do to make them feel greater loyalty and commitment to your goals?

Building relationships, however, is not always easy. Cheryl's progress was difficult; she had moments of real doubt and uncertainty. She recognized that she needed other people to help her so that she could develop and motivate her team.

Cheryl is convinced that she was successful because of three key factors. First, her boss was 100 percent behind her. Second, she had an internal consultant who became a trusted sounding board for her ideas and her pain, assisting her through the change and the maze of hostility. And, third, she hired a trusted administrative assistant from her previous assignment within the organization. So, on a day-to-day basis, she had relationships with other people who helped her. She trusted them and could rely on them for support as she developed and strengthened her relationship with her team.

Networking: The Basics

Many relationships begin from the process of networking. This overused word often conjures up images of people running around passing out business cards. For the sake of clarity, here's my definition: Networking is the act of building mutually beneficial relationships with people who can in some way support your personal and professional development and assist you in achieving your goals.

Networking enables you to meet a variety of people who can help you by sharing information and knowledge with you. In fact, I recommend that you set up "knowledge-sharing meetings" with people you have identified as having knowledge and information that is critical to your success. These meetings don't have to be anything formal, just simple requests to meet over coffee, lunch, or a drink after work for the purpose of sharing information and knowledge.

As you get to know people and build relationships with them, you'll be able to get and give support and feedback. In the process, you'll be expanding your visibility; the more visibility you have, the more exposure you'll have to opportunities. As your network of relationships grows, your own sphere of influence and credibility will expand and you'll have greater chances of being invited into special circles of influence and meeting potential mentors and role models. Some networking gurus say that networking is the most cost-effective way to market yourself, but I like to think of it as a way to grow as a leader by developing mutually satisfying relationships.

In the business world, there are myriad places to go to network and meet people. In addition to people inside your company, there are professional associations, meetings, trade shows, and industry conferences you can attend. You can network with colleagues and bosses from past jobs, former clients and customers, vendors and suppliers. Outside of the professional arena, there are plenty of community, social, and church groups, as well as family and friends. Decide which organizations to join and which events to attend, and realize that these might change over time as you grow or your career develops. But in networking, remember to be strategic—it's quality, not quantity that counts.

Network with Conscious Intent

As you develop your networking strategy, remain focused on your vision and goals as you decide whom you want to meet and how you can meet them. Go places and meet people with the conscious intent of developing strategic connections. This is such an easy step, but I often find myself falling short even when my own experience tells me how beneficial it is to go somewhere with the intent of getting to meet someone who can help me.

Let me give you an example of what I mean—several years ago I went to a meeting of a professional group with the clear intent to meet someone from Verizon. I knew the company was a leader in bringing women up through the management ranks, and I wanted an entrée. Before I left for the event, I focused on achieving a successful outcome, and visualized how it would go. Lo and behold, the person who sat down beside me at the meeting was a Verizon HR manager! She ended up connecting me with one of the leaders of the Women's Association for Verizon Employees (WAVE) in Boston. I was soon hired to conduct two workshops for this group, who then passed my name on to the WAVE group in Maryland. Six months later, I conducted a workshop for them. Other times I go to a gathering without taking the time to reflect on my needs and my vision, and I leave feeling unfulfilled, not having made connections that count.

Presenting with Presence

When you meet people in networking situations, it's critical to present yourself as credible and powerful. Even if you don't feel powerful, move out of your comfort zone and act as though you are, because *perception counts*. When I met Sydney Rice Harrild (whom I mentioned earlier), I had no idea that she wasn't satisfied with her space in the corner. All I saw was a poised, friendly woman who stood out from the crowd—someone with enough self-confidence to position herself in a unique way. My first impression of Sydney as a well-put-together businesswoman was based only on her demeanor and attire. This impression was later reinforced by the quality of her business materials. So, whether you're networking inside or outside your organization, create ways to make yourself visible and to demonstrate your credibility and the quality of your work.

Networking requires self-confidence and assertiveness. I found Sydney because she assertively moved herself into a better highly trafficked position at the conference we were attending. She repositioned herself so that she could bring her message to more women. If she hadn't, I might not have seen her, because I was busy selling books at my own table. And, if I hadn't asserted myself and had enough self-confidence to follow up, we wouldn't have the relationship that we do.

The Elevator Speech

When you are networking, many times you will only have a few minutes to catch people's attention and get them to see your value. Therefore, you need to have a good handle on that time-honored tool—the "elevator speech." Your elevator speech should describe what is unique about you. It should be short, catchy, and memorable, and include interesting work you have been doing, particular skills and talents that you have, and possibly your goals. You want it to draw the attention of the other person and make them curious to learn more about you. You will only have a short amount of time to do this (the time it takes for an elevator to travel from one floor to the next—hence the name), so have your speech down pat. This is why it's critical to know yourself, your skills and strengths, and know what you bring to the table. You should have your speech "in your body" so that it easily rolls out off of your tongue. You don't necessarily have to memorize it, but you should have practiced it out loud often enough to have "cell" memory of it—at a moment's notice, you should know what to say and how to say it, depending on whom you are meeting.

Sometimes you might not be sure how to approach an individual whom you are interested in getting to know professionally. One approach is to start by pointing out something that you admire about the person, such as his expertise or accomplishments or how he developed his career. You might ask him if he has time to meet or have a conversation on the phone so that you can get advice from him. Another approach is to point out similarities between you or how you can support each other. Ask if he would like to explore possible professional synergies between the two of you. Again, suggest getting together or having a conversation on the phone. If you are calling or e-mailing an individual who has been referred to you by a third party, mention your contact right away so that you immediately establish a connection.

Your Elevator Speech

Write a two- or three-sentence elevator speech describing yourself and what is unique about you. Try to include some of your goals. Remember it should arouse curiosity and catch the attention of the other person.

Practice saying it out loud. Then ask a couple of colleagues to practice with you as you shake hands, look them in the eye, and introduce yourself. Listen to their feedback about what you need to do to be even better at introducing yourself.

Another smart networking technique is to simply conduct informational interviews on the phone. Be prepared to clearly state your reason for wanting the interview, and ask intelligent questions. This is a good strategy for introducing yourself to senior managers you might not otherwise have an opportunity to meet. One of the executives I interviewed for *Success on Our Own Terms* used this technique repeatedly to gain visibility with senior management and build her corporate career.

Building Relationships: Focus on the Other Person

When you're networking, be sure to focus on the other person. Ask people open-ended questions about themselves and their work, and actively listen to what they say. Be generous by offering your support and asking how you can be of help to them.

Don't be as concerned about giving your business card as getting one from them. Make notations on the cards to remind yourself who the person is and what his or her interests are so that you can refer to it when you follow up. When you do follow up, frame your next conversation in a way that engages the other person and draws his interest. Know what you want from the contact, and know what you have to offer. I wanted to meet with Sydney in person because I wanted more time to learn how she managed her business and structured her coaching practice. At the time, I didn't know Sydney was interested in writing a book. But since she was a coach, I thought she might be interested in what I had learned about women in business. Therefore, when I introduced myself on the phone, I emphasized my research and writing.

Networking Do's and Don'ts	
Do think strategically, and design your approach.	Don't focus on quantity over quality.
Do communicate your value and uniqueness.	Don't make assumptions about what people know or who they are.
Do demonstrate your credibility and power.	Don't give a limp handshake.
Do ask open-ended, powerful questions.	Don't center the conversation on you.
Do focus on the other person.	Don't forget to help the other person.
Do listen actively.	Don't only talk to the people you know at events.
Do carry business cards.	Don't stay with one person too long at events.
Do close with confidence.	Don't force your business card on others.
Do get the other person's business card.	Don't load your hands and mouth with food and drink.
Do follow up.	Don't stay too long in your comfort zone.

Remember that networking takes time. It's like cultivating a garden. In order to get beautiful flowers or luscious vegetables and fruits, you must first fertilize the ground, then plant the seeds, and then water and weed. It takes nurturing, care, attention, and time, but the benefits are worth the effort. With a full garden of great people to pick from, you'll find yourself rewarded by your relationships.

Strategic Relationships Summary Steps

This final strategy for coaching yourself to leadership requires planning, thoughtfulness, and a deep attitude of respect, and it calls for competency in the previous four strategies. Before you can build strategic alliances and supportive relationships, you have to know yourself. When you're interacting with others, you'll discover that the most rewarding relationships develop when you are authentic and true to yourself. In order to determine who possesses the skills and connections to help you, you'll need to have an understanding of what you want and where you want to go. You'll also have to be an effective communicator who knows how to clearly articulate your strengths, uniqueness, and goals, and who knows how to listen actively to others to deepen understanding and build trust. Your strategic relationships will be further enriched and will become even more beneficial to you if you operate from an emotionally intelligent place—a place from which both you and others can learn and grow.

As you think about the relationships that are important to you, remember to understand what each requires from you. How your team perceives you and how your boss perceives you will be critical to your success as a leader. Although trust is the core foundation for building all relationships, how you build a relationship with your boss will differ from the way you build relationships with your peers, mentors, and direct reports. Different relationships will call for different ways of communicating, influencing, and motivating. Throughout this process, it's essential for you to think strategically about who is critical to your development and what is the best way to connect with them. Mentors are especially important, and you'll want to form relationships with various mentors throughout your career.

Building relationships will require you to develop your networking skills, and you might need to step out of your comfort zone as you reach out to people you don't know. This calls for you to present yourself in an enticing and credible way. As you form productive relationships with key players, as you expand your network of connections inside and outside your organization, and as you build a committed, high-performance team, you'll be enhancing your leadership skills. As you enhance your own skills, don't forget to turn around and mentor other people below and around you. The more quality relationships you develop and nurture, the more opportunities you'll have to learn and grow as a leader.

Coaching Questions on Strategic Relationships

Answer the following questions, reflecting on what you need to do to build strategic relationships.

With whom do you need to build a relationship? What kind of alliances do you need? What characteristics are important to you in potential alliance partners?

Where will you find these people? How will you arrange to meet them? How can each of these people contribute to your success?

What do you have to offer them? What will you say to them that will elicit their interest in you?

What challenges might you encounter in your efforts to network and build alliances? How can you overcome them?

What do you need to do to remain true to yourself while you develop strategic relationships?

How can you maintain and nurture relationships with bosses, mentors, team members, peers, and direct reports?

(continued)

| Coaching Questions on |
| Strategic Relationships *(concluded)* |

How approachable are you? What can you do to be more approachable?

How much do people trust you? What can you do to build trust?

How effective is your team? What do you need to do to be a better leader for your team?

How good is your relationship with your boss? What can you do to make it better?

How often do you mentor others? What are you willing to commit to regarding mentoring?

What kind of leadership "presence" do you have? What do you need to do to enhance it?

Conclusion

Now the hard part begins: putting what you've learned from reading this book into practice every day. As I said earlier, growth as a leader is an ongoing, iterative process. It requires you to examine yourself on a continual basis, to be honest with yourself, and to be committed to your own development. Sometimes you will fail and make mistakes.

That's okay. What's important is to understand why you made the mistake so that you can learn how to be different the next time you encounter a similar situation. I hope that by exposing my own mistakes, you will learn from them. And I hope that you have been inspired by the success stories of the people I've worked with, who found ways to improve their leadership abilities and stretch themselves to achieve their goals.

Business and organizational success is dependent on the quality of leadership present in the organization. At every level, organizations require strong, integrated leaders who know how to manage themselves, their people, and their business. Organizations need leaders who know themselves and understand others. They want leaders who know where to go, how to get there, and how to communicate their vision, mission, and strategy to others, engaging and motivating employees to achieve organizational goals. Organizations must also have leaders who appreciate the importance of alliances and understand on a very deep level that it is only through mutually beneficial relationships with other quality people and groups that the organization can find success.

I'm surprised at what people don't understand about themselves and others. Leadership can be taught, and the earlier it's taught, the more value it can add. We ought to be teaching human development, psychology, and communication skills starting in kindergarten so that people grow up with more knowledge about themselves and what it takes to interact with others in emotionally healthy ways. The more we can educate people about what it means to be a leader and how to acquire those skills, the more opportunity we'll have to create strong, successful organizations. At the moment, we don't seem to have that type of curriculum in our elementary and secondary schools—at least not in the

United States. Therefore, as adults, we need to educate ourselves in whatever way possible. I hope *Coaching Yourself to Leadership* has given you tools to coach yourself so that you can continue your learning and leadership development and become an integrated leader who can lead yourself and others toward success, happiness, and fulfillment.

About the Author

Ginny O'Brien, MS, PCC, is an executive and corporate coach, specializing in leadership development and women's advancement. In 1998, she founded The Columbia Consultancy, a leadership development coaching firm. She has worked with managers, directors, and executives—both men and women—from Fortune 500 corporations as well as small- and medium-sized companies.

A skilled facilitator and workshop leader, Ginny has presented at major conferences and led workshops for over 100 organizations. She is the author of two other books: *Success on Our Own Terms: Tales of Extraordinary, Ordinary Business Women* (John Wiley, 1998), which provides strategies for navigating the corporate world and best practices for women's initiatives and advancing women in management, and *The Fast Forward MBA in Business* (John Wiley, 1996), which is an easy-to-read reference guide to business principles and management theory that has been translated into six languages. In addition, she was a contributing author to *Winning in the New Europe: Taking Advantage of the Single Market* (Prentice Hall, 1992), and her articles on business intelligence and career strategies have been published in the business and trade press. Ginny has been featured in major newspapers, has appeared on regional and national radio and TV shows, and is listed in the *International Who's Who of Professional and Business Women*.

Ginny holds a summa cum laude BA in psychology and an MS in communication. She is a Professional Certified Coach (PCC) with the International Coach Federation and a Certified Professional Behavioral Analyst (CPBA). She lives in Marblehead, Massachusetts, and can be reached at ginny@ginnyobrien.com or through her Web site at www.ginnyobrien.com.